WRITE TO SHOOT

Write to Shoot teaches budding screenwriters and screenwriting filmmakers how to write a short script with production in mind. Beker instructs them on how to showcase their strengths, tailor projects to shoestring budgets, resources, and practical production parameters without sacrificing the quality and punch of their screenplays, whether they're creating a sizzle short for an unproduced feature script, an independent creative work, or a soapbox to promote a cause. *Write to Shoot: Writing Short Films for Production* is a must-have guide for anyone who wants to be sure there will be no surprises on set that come from a script that's not ready for production.

Marilyn Beker is a professor of screenwriting in the School of Film and Television at Loyola Marymount University in Los Angeles, California. She is the author of *Screenwriting With a Conscience: Ethics for Screenwriters* and *The Screenwriter Activist: Writing Social Issue Movies*. She has extensive screenwriting and production experience and is the recipient of the Visionary Leader in Education Award from Shorts HD and Shorts International for her work in short films.

WRITE TO SHOOT

Writing Short Films for Production

Marilyn Beker

NEW YORK AND LONDON

First published 2017
by Routledge
711 Third Avenue, New York, NY 10017

and by Routledge
2 Park Square, Milton Park, Abingdon, Oxon OX14 4RN

Routledge is an imprint of the Taylor & Francis Group, an informa business

© 2017 Taylor & Francis

The right of Marilyn Beker to be identified as the author of this work has been asserted by her in accordance with sections 77 and 78 of the Copyright, Designs and Patents Act 1988.

All rights reserved. No part of this book may be reprinted or reproduced or utilised in any form or by any electronic, mechanical, or other means, now known or hereafter invented, including photocopying and recording, or in any information storage or retrieval system, without permission in writing from the publishers.

Trademark notice: Product or corporate names may be trademarks or registered trademarks, and are used only for identification and explanation without intent to infringe.

Library of Congress Cataloging-in-Publication Data
Names: Beker, Marilyn, author.
Title: Write to shoot : writing short films for production / Marilyn Beker.
Description: New York ; London : Routledge, Taylor & Francis Group, 2017. | Includes bibliographical references and index.
Identifiers: LCCN 2016040757 (print) | LCCN 2017001462 (ebook) | ISBN 9781138844629 (hardback : alk. paper) | ISBN 9781138844636 (pbk. : alk. paper) | ISBN 9781315730219 (ebk.)
Subjects: LCSH: Motion picture authorship.
Classification: LCC PN1996 .B4535 2017 (print) | LCC PN1996 (ebook) | DDC 809.2/3—dc23
LC record available at https://lccn.loc.gov/2016040757

ISBN: 978-1-138-84462-9 (hbk)
ISBN: 978-1-138-84463-6 (pbk)
ISBN: 978-1-315-73021-9 (ebk)

Typeset in ITC New Baskerville
by Apex CoVantage, LLC

For
J. Oliver Black

CONTENTS

Preface		viii
Acknowledgments		xii
Introduction		xiv
1	Why?	1
2	What?	11
3	The Short Answer	22
4	The Short Bible	32
5	Money Changes Everything	76
6	Killing Your Darlings	97
7	Budget Tourniquets	112
8	The Shooting Script	122
9	Your Type	129
10	Bankroll	146
11	Getting Seen	156
12	Be a Ninja!	168

PREFACE

Screenwriters are big dreamers. We love writing down those dreams so they can be made "real." Wanting to see what's in our heads made universally visible is what drives us. It's a tall order but one we've signed up for. And we usually wait with the hope that someone will share our dream and actually commit to producing it.

Sometimes that's a long wait. Often we're rebuffed and rejected. Sick of that? Well, there's another way around this waiting game, and that's to make the film ourselves. Those of us ready to take this giant step of actually materializing our dreams by shooting them are faced with an even more daunting dilemma. We need to become practical, and in dreamland, practicality is a four-letter word that often tears us apart. We're afraid that we'll be forced by the exigencies of that practicality to minimize our vision so drastically that it'll become ordinary, predictable, oversimple, and banal. We're terrified of having to mess with technology we don't understand, and we're afraid to trust those who do understand it to get our vision right. We're scared that our project will be way too expensive. And those are just a few of the hideous fears that drum into our brain as we go forward.

Well, help is on the way. This book was written to allay those fears by showing writers who want to make their own movies how to overcome challenges that give rise to terrors. The secret of that overcoming is anticipating the problems that may come up on set and eliminating them as the script is written.

Ideally, all scripts should be written this way, but they aren't. When writers are working on spec feature scripts, we let our imaginations run wild. And rightly so. We aren't thinking of budget and logistics because we hope and pray some studio/production company with big bucks will snap up our project and run with it. That's a legitimate way to go if you're into big-budget movies.

Those of us who are tired of hoping and praying and want to put our work out there ourselves often decide to write low-budget films. And when we do, we need to consider things a bit more carefully. We usually tailor our stories to be "smaller," more compact, and less involved. And those of us who want to make short films as sizzle reels for our features (high and low budgets) and as calling cards for our talent are faced with being even more stringent in what we write.

But how do we do that without losing our initial creative burst, gutting our story, or dreaming small? That's the challenge. We've got to write smart, solve puzzles, and become savvy connoisseurs of the filmmaking art. We've got to better understand how to write for production!

That's because we need to accept the fact that what we write won't get realized if no one can figure out how to pay for it or shoot it.

We've got to know at our core that we're involved in a limited (for now) medium that involves equipment, wires, gadgets, and all manner of technology with which some of us may be uncomfortable. We've got to learn to acknowledge that we need that technology to get our vision out there, and we've got to learn how to work in ways that will allow that technology to be easily applied. This is a huge challenge to lots of screenwriters who would prefer not to deal with technology at all (apart from their own computers and sometimes—God forbid you're using a quill!—not even those). That's why it's important as we write to think about production issues that may come up.

Often, too many people start writing without thinking about these kinds of issues. They say they'll do that after they have the script. This is dangerous and a waste of time. Unless the script you plan to produce is written with production in mind, lots of changes will need to be made during shooting, and that can create nightmare situations. Better to think of technical logistics before and during writing.

To do that, many of us have to overcome our fear of technology. We're afraid because there are so many buttons, knobs, and things that can go wrong. The solution to all of this is simple. Partner up with someone who likes gadgets. And if you can't do that, get yourself equipment that is laughingly simple and learn to use it: iPhones, iPads, really easy point-and-shoot cameras.

These may have what we might consider quality drawbacks (I hear purists whine that the quality isn't as good as film, etc.) but forget about that. If the important thing is the message and story you want to get across, then lower some of your standards! The reality is that if the story is compelling, people will forgive the odd technical glitch. You just have to make sure it can be heard well (sound is paramount) and actually seen . . . not too dark or too light.

That's what this book will help you do. Sure you may need to compromise a little, but that little compromise is what's going to get the pictures you have in your head come to life on the screen (and maybe someday in holographs . . . right in front of people. Even as I write this Microsoft is releasing a holographic lens—Microsoft HoloLens—that, as Microsoft's site tells us, "blends holograms with reality." Wow. Imagine the possibilities!).

Remember—compromise isn't always a bad word. Purists will tell you that it is and that no real artist who is true to herself should compromise. Poppycock. All art is compromise at some level. For instance, the medium in which artists work forces compromise. Painters have to give in to the demands of watercolors oils, pigments, and potions. Screenwriters have to say things clearly in order to be understood by the people charged with physically mounting the movie. That means, of course, that screenwriters have to adhere to a very strict format that isn't always satisfying (think of the leeway novelists have to include thoughts and emotions and bits of philosophy). Screenwriters can only deal with what is directly seen or heard. But that's what, for me, makes the screenwriting puzzle fun. It's challenging to create something that will transmit thoughts and philosophy without resorting to blatant exposition.

That's also what makes screenwriting hard. And particularly so when it involves making those things real when there are so many other things to think about . . . location, action, dialogue, character development, sequencing, structure. The list goes on.

And for those of us who plan on shooting our own projects, the biggest concern is budget! How to fit all we want to do into a circumscribed budget arena is perhaps most daunting of all. But it doesn't have to be. Think of fashion. Lots of us would love to wear couture worth thousands (a Dior jacket with a $24,000 price tag would be nice!), but with a little ingenuity and flare, we can figure out how to get the look for much, much less (think knock-off Dior retail for maybe $78.00!) It can be done, and I admit I do it! The same is true for film. We can find ways to reduce the amount we spend by ingenious ways. Some of those ways we'll discuss in detail later.

So here's to the daring adventure that is writing for production. It's the first part of a bigger dream, and it's exciting because if we do it right we can lay the groundwork for finally seeing our mind movie on screen and have certainty and control in the process.

ACKNOWLEDGMENTS

This book is all about being practical—applying what we know in ways that will work. It took me lots of time to learn that, and I'm grateful to my teacher J. Oliver Black for impressing upon me how important that was. In addition to that, he also encouraged me to be creative and bold and above all to enjoy every moment of my life no matter what! That's a tall order, but I've tried to do that and want to thank some of the people who helped me find joy in all things. Huge thanks to my husband Greg Rorabaugh, partner in the cosmic frolic, to my late parents Bronia and Joseph Beker who gave me so much, my indomitable sister Jeanne Beker, my talented nieces Joey O'Neil and Bekky O'Neil and to the extended family and friends I'm blessed to have in my life; the Rorabaughs, the Del Principes, Iain Macinnes, Ruth, Alan and Noah Ickowitz, Chana and Aaron Solomon, Margie Friedman, Irene and Juliette Gringeri, Carol and Richard Armour, John and Ann Pfluecke, the old Ranch hands, Karen Jones, Maggie and Hymie Milstein, Bob Nankin, Ann Kimber, Kelly O'Hara, Vanessa M. Coto, Cherilyn Camero, Rosemary Massey, life saver Dr. Devora Cohen, and as always, PY, SY, LM, B, K, DM and Brother Saralananda. Thanks to LMU design student and now alum Emma Tung for the cover design, to Thomas Ethan Harris for his festival wisdom, to Robbie Colangelo for her crowdfunding expertise, to the gifted Ebony Gilbert for her case study and to Shorts HD and Shorts International, particularly the dynamic Marshall Nord for their promotion of short films and their generosity to me and to my students. Thanks to Jeffrey Davis for his support and kindness, to Loyola Marymount University and to all my students over the years who taught me so much and continue to do so every day. Thanks also to Erica Wetter at Routledge for seeing the worth in this book. Finally, I applaud the ongoing work of the technical geniuses who make it possible for all of us to film our stories in new ways.

INTRODUCTION

Aren't all screenplays written for production? Theoretically that's true because screenplays are blueprints filmmakers follow to make movies. The problem is that all scripts (long and short) start out as literary reads to garner interest and attract funding. The "real" work comes when the project is green-lit and then often, horrible things happen to the script that started it all.

That's because screenwriters usually aren't writing with production parameters in mind and filmmakers who write their own scripts are too busy getting their ideas down to think of production "yet," or if they are thinking of production, their scripts are so technical that the story gets lost. This doesn't have to happen. The screenwriter can get control and make the hand-off process less painful and the screenwriting filmmaker can be more prepared by writing specifically to production issues while getting the story across and so save time and headaches on set.

This book is for motivated screenwriters and filmmakers who already know the basics of screenwriting and who want to write and shoot a short film in order to learn the craft of film making and/or promote themselves to the industry. Too often talented screenwriters and screenwriting filmmakers languish in obscurity because they have trouble getting people to read their material or recognize that material's potential. If a screenwriter or filmmaker can demonstrate skill and talent by producing an attention-getting short project, that person's visibility grows exponentially as people take a quick look and take notice.

In the succeeding chapters you'll learn how to write a script with production in mind by embedding production particulars in the actual literary script; how to manage story and story particulars to coincide with budget, resources, and practical production parameters without losing the punch and power of a literary screenplay; and how to showcase your strengths and tailor projects to your specific career goals. Look at it as a must-have guide for anyone who wants to be sure there will be no surprises on set that come from a script not ready for production!

We'll deal exclusively with shorts for several reasons. Film schools require students to make shorts to satisfy degree requirements. New platforms (cell phones, the Internet) demand short content. Cable companies and networks now have channels specifically devoted to shorts, and online short films are gaining increasing credibility as gateways to broader career options in the entertainment industry. Short films serve as calling cards and talent showcases for writers, directors, editors, cinematographers, actors, and story tellers in general.

1
WHY?

Tolstoy, in his book *What Is Art?*, explores artistic motives at the very onset of the work. He asks probing questions that all artists (and filmmakers are most definitely artists) need to ask themselves at the onset of careers or projects. The first of these comes down to "is it worth it?" That's because he admits that art demands tremendous labor and sacrifices on the part of the artist and goes so far as to say that the making of it stunts human lives and transgresses against human love (Tolstoy, 2005, Chapter 1).

The clear answer, the one that bears no excuses, is that we do art because we have to. Something inside us compels us, and without doing it we can't exist. This is the most basic and legitimate reason for making art. That applies, of course, to our writing, but does it also apply to our actually making the movie? That's a more complicated question.

I admit that I was never wild about the production process. For me, writing was so much simpler . . . just me and a computer and my head. No wires, no equipment, no people to get in the way. And these things all do get in the way. It always amazes me that the production process is as complicated as it is. I'm certain in the future everything will be wireless and equipment simple . . . in fact, I dream about some time when we will simply sit down at some kind of machine and have it scan our mind as we think up movies that will automatically download onto a screen. Ah the glories of science fiction! Because I was born too soon, that isn't possible right now. And so the complicated mess that is production takes over and often makes an even bigger mess of the wonderful movies we see in our heads.

The translation of thought into form is always a hassle. Think of the inventor who keeps making prototype after prototype to get his invention right and working. The movies we make are certainly prototypes, but alas, these "prototypes" can't be easily scrapped. They are too expensive and too public. We've got to make them as good as they can be, and we've got to make them good enough for a market to accept. This is no easy task. And naturally, it's a given that the movie we make is NEVER as good as the movie we thought of in the first place.

In order to get the thing made at all, we've got to first do some serious and often scary gymnastics that far outweigh the writing process. By creating a budget based on our script, we've got to figure out how much our movie will cost us to produce using software we might not be familiar with. That means the first step is to get familiar with Movie Magic or some other kind of budgeting software we can get our hands on. Once we have a budget, we've got to raise that money.

And then the real work begins...we've got to scout locations, lock them down, get permits, cast the picture, get equipment, solicit crew members (production designers, camera people, set builders, lighting experts, sound people, grips, etc.)... the list seems endless. And, of course, unless you can get these people to work for free (film schools are great places for just that reason!) you're in for a whole lot of wallet opening.

Then we've got to actually shoot the thing in keeping with a schedule based on our script that we've made up beforehand (also to be mastered in software). And when we're through with all of that, we've got to edit the rough footage and make sure the sound is perfect.

Finally, we've got to send the film to festivals, enter online contests and bang our drums in hopes of getting distribution. And if we're lucky to garner some interest, we've got to parlay our movie into our next project. I'm exhausted just writing about this.

That's why we've got to be sure that we really, really want to make this movie. To do that, we've got to examine our motives. Are we in it for the money? Well, there is NO money until we get it distributed and shown, but even then there may be little or no return, especially with a short. Because shorts are used as calling cards or sizzle reels, they are simply gateways to our next project.

If we are lucky enough to license shorts to a distributor, we will make only about $18 a minute total running time, plus 20 Euros a minute total running time if it also shows in Europe, etc., for a three-year period. This is fabulous if you can get it because your film will be seen and you may be noticed, but it means for a 15-minute film, the most you can make is about $600 (the Euro fluctuates so the figure is not exact).

It quickly becomes obvious that money is a poor motive indeed. If that's your primary motive, your energy will usually flag when you do the budget and discover how behind the eight ball you are when it gets to just mounting the thing and how little profit there is for you in this budget raising. You can, of course, include a "salary" for yourself in that budget, but usually you don't because that's an overhead that will keep you that many dollars away from making the thing. Often, the above-the-line costs (writer, director, producer, composer) are the first budget items to go in order to trim down how much you'll need to raise to get the project off the ground. So forget the money motive. It will make you quit before you start.

The fame motive? Ha! You won't get famous until the movie makes some kind of mark and you get a feature made and even then, nobody might know you. Unfortunately, the people who get noticed are the stars of your movie and usually not the director. Especially not the writer! There's that old Hollywood joke about the starlet who wanted a part in a picture and made a huge mistake by sleeping with the writer! As everyone knows, writers have really no power in the industry unless they start to be bankable. Then they can move to director status or command huge bucks for their work. But they are still obscure rascals who have trouble getting tables at good restaurants.

Fame's a lousy reason. I know that you don't believe that fame can be a burden, but trust me it's no picnic. If you do happen to get famous, your life will change drastically. No more walking down the street incognito. No more hanging out at your favorite coffee shop. No more shopping for groceries. Every moment your life will be plagued by paparazzi and hangers-on. Of course, some of you might relish this thought, but take it from me, it can be invasive and downright creepy.

In my own life, I know firsthand what that's like. My sister, Jeanne Beker, is a famous media star in Canada and parts of Europe. She gets recognized and greeted everyplace she goes. And the freebies she gets are great . . . complementary desserts and drinks at restaurants, the best tables, the kindness of strangers . . . but it's not always great. For example, we were at a restaurant and about to take our first bite of lunch when two people showed up and asked for a picture with my sister. She graciously put her fork down, got up, and complied. Then they insisted she go outside with them and take a bunch of pictures for an album they were putting together. Some nerve! But the worst was when our father was dying in the hospital. We were sitting in the private waiting room, devastated, when a woman barged in, ran up to my sister, and ignoring all our tears, yammered on about getting an autograph! A most horrible and distressing moment. But, of course, if you're craving fame none of this will mean anything to you. So if that's your motive, prepare to wait a long time to get it. If you have patience, that may be a good motive, but it doesn't cut it when you're broke, eating Top Ramen, and spending all your time in the editing room!

So what motivation does work? Passion! Passion for your future, passion for your art, passion for the story you need to tell, and passion for the process. In an interview with me, Marshall Nord, president of Shorts HD, said,

> *[P]assion will get you through all those sleepless nights of work. If you think you can spend your time doing anything other than your short film then go do it because you're going to get chewed up. It's not an easy process. Now that being said, it weeds people out but go into it with your eyes wide open and lots of passion.*

That and commitment will take you a long way. Belief in yourself and your story is all you really have, and if you have that, you have it all. But keep in mind that in addition to that passion you've also got to be able to commit. Because the filmmaking process is so rigorous and demanding, you've got to make a commitment to yourself and your story early on. If you don't do that, you won't end up making a film at all.

For example, I had a student in my graduate thesis class who was both brilliant and talented. He had ideas coming out of his ears and was a fabulous writer. But he was also a neurotic commitment-phobe.

At the start of the class I ask students to come up with three ideas for a short film that will become their final thesis project. This student came up with 40 ideas! And what's worse, he couldn't commit to any of them. He made himself (and the rest of the class) crazy worrying about which project was "worthy," and finally when I put my foot down and made him choose one, he kept on writing different versions of it. When he was asked to do one short script of no more than 15 pages, he wrote six different scripts on the same subject of 40 pages each! I was boiling with frustration but so was he. He kept wanting me to tell him which movie would "work" best, but unfortunately in filmmaking there are no guarantees.

We work through the story and the script, developing it as best we can, until we get a draft we must commit to and bring into the production process. But we can't do that until we first commit to the idea and to the script.

Finally, that student was able to commit to a script that was 17 pages long. Only trouble was that he wrote three versions of that one. In the end he had to be threatened with failure that would have prevented him from shooting his graduate thesis project in order to make him commit to a final version. And even then, I believe he truly didn't commit to it. He hasn't made the film yet, but I predict that the production process will be nearly impossible for him because he has trouble making decisions (obviously), and making decisions is what screenwriting and directing and production is all about.

In fact, making decisions is what art is all about. The artist makes decisions based on an inner feeling, on an insight, or on a sense of proportion or "rightness." Slightly different versions may be trotted out, but each variation finally gets closer to the real and right one. The refining process takes place in smaller and smaller increments where areas are reworked and "fixed." It doesn't take place by continually throwing out projects and starting anew. Sometimes, throwing a project out is necessary, but only after the revision process has been exhausted, and even then I'm not sure that it's a smart move. Sometimes artists get lazy and frustrated and sick of what they are working on. That's a sign that they need to back away for a while until they can look at the project with fresh eyes. It can take weeks, months, or even years.

Often, coming back to a project after a long time makes you realize that it was pretty good after all. And if not, the time away makes seeing the places that can be fixed clearer.

The important thing is to stay with the core of the story. I get lots of students who want to quit after a few revisions or when they come up with something they think is insurmountable. I tell them that nothing is insurmountable and that the answer is in there somewhere. They just need to tackle it with new eyes and insight, and sometimes that takes fortitude and stick-to-it-ness. My motto is never give up! If you believe in the project, and if you are convinced it's a story that needs to be told, there is always a way to make it work.

So you need to commit to your idea and your script. You may have doubts—that's only natural—but until you have a story you love and a script you can make ready for production, you are nowhere.

Motivation Analysis Exercise

Here's a little exercise you can use to help you determine your motivation and whether it's strong enough to help you survive the writing and production process.

1. Be honest. List all the reasons you have for making this movie.
2. Look over the list and beside each reason put a number out of 100 that reflects how strong that reason is. For example, money: 75, fame 20, love 90, getting Hugo to love and notice me 100, and so on.
3. Now look at each reason and analyze honestly what result you might expect, that is, the return on your energy investment in that particular reason. For example, if Hugo never noticed you, it may be likely that he will notice you when he sees the movie. But realistically, if he didn't love you before, it's very

unlikely that your movie will make him flip out over you. And if it does and that's the only reason he loves you, he's a shallow lad indeed.

It's important that you are extremely realistic during this process. No cheating or dreaming.

Hurdles Exercise

Once your motivation is clear, consider the hurdles you will have to jump to get the movie made.

1. Write down all the skills you need and have to make this movie.
2. Write down all the skills you need but don't have to make this movie.
3. Write down the people in your life who will be affected (and to what degree) by your involvement in this work.

This portion of the exercise is important because it will affect your entire life and well-being.

1. If, for example, you are married with three kids and have decided to quit your job to make this movie or mortgage your house, your significant other may not be too thrilled. Will that person be okay with having to earn all the money and do all the chores, etc., to keep your household afloat?
2. Will your significant other be okay with you working with members of the opposite sex for hours on end, or is that person insanely jealous and/r insecure?
3. Will your parents be okay with you moving back home and spending all your money on this project?
4. Can you stand not spending an extra cent on anything else like entertainment, incidentals, and fun?

5. If you don't succeed and the project goes belly up, will you be okay with losing lots of time and money?
6. Can you live with failure and flops?
7. Can you handle being laughed at, scorned, ridiculed, or misunderstood?
8. Can you handle being lauded, applauded, and revered? (This may seem easier than handling flops, but in reality, it can be just as devastating in different ways.)
9. Do you have enough good friends and contacts to help you make your movie?
10. Can you call in favors and are you good at getting deals?
11. Do you have the physical stamina, energy, and good health to push yourself to the limits?
12. Do you have a good sense of humor?
13. Can you solve problems quickly?
14. Are you a take-charge person?
15. Do you get overwhelmed easily?
16. Are you too hard on yourself?
17. Are you too demanding of others?
18. Are you too demanding of yourself?
19. Are you a practical person?
20. Are you realistic?
21. Do you have some understanding of human nature and technology?
22. Are you forward thinking and good at anticipating needs?

All of these are psychological mine fields that, if ignored, will mess you up in the production process for sure and, yes, in the writing process as well. Because when you write with production in mind, you need to be able to create doable scenarios that you can visualize working. And you need to have the confidence to know that you can get them to work in spite of messy circumstances and problems that might come up.

Writing for production is about anticipating problems and solving them in script, and taking that script into production sometimes requires adjustments and even more problem solving. If you don't have the personality that can cope with whatever is thrown at you, then perhaps, as Tolstoy says, making this kind of art is not for you. Better to know that before you start than at the end of a long and painful process that might devastate you, your finances, and your family.

If you haven't thrown this book down and run screaming from the room, if you've carefully analyzed yourself and seen that you are up for the task, it's time to get busy and find your story.

Reference

Tolstoy, Leo. *What Is Art?* New York: Barnes and Noble, 2005.

2
WHAT?

Finding Your Story

What's real? Back when the Beatles sang "Strawberry Fields," they said "nothing is real," and if you're hooked into Eastern philosophy or a fan of the esoteric or a physicist, you might already realize that everything is nothing more than a bunch of particles zooming around congealed in space, which is also a bunch of particles . . . well, it goes on and on. Knowing this presents a considerable challenge to those of us who want to create a piece of art that will feel real to audiences and authentic enough to move them in some way.

The thing we've got to see is that the reality we express is our own version of things. In that way, everything we say or do is incredibly personal. All the stories we tell are filtered through our own personal lenses—lenses that are influenced or even created by our past experiences, our perceptions, our interests, our proclivities, our beliefs. We can't get away from that no matter how hard we try. Even documentaries and news stories come to us via people who interpret these events for us. Even live camera footage of events is biased simply by the angle from which the footage is taken. The person holding the camera directs the lens in certain ways, moves the camera in certain ways, and stops and starts at certain points. And although those actions seem beyond subtle, nevertheless they have some influence on the telling of the visual story and even the contextual one.

I learned this early on listening to my parents tell stories about their experiences during World War II and comparing them with the stories their friends told. These stories, so personal and powerful, were divergent enough to make me wonder if everyone was talking about the same war. And, of course, that's true even today when we hear reports of current wars. Depending on the outlet telling the story, we get our information through particular political and social biases. This is an obvious and well-known fact by now. (Read McLuhan and other media theorists and even outlets themselves that blatantly advertise their points of view. Think Al Jazeera, NPR, CNBC.)

During my freshman year in college, I interned as a teenage cub reporter working the night rewrite desk of Canada's then-largest newspaper *The Toronto Star*. This was in the Jurassic age when there were no computers, cell phones, or fax machines. Oh the horror! So that meant that correspondents around the world would phone their stories into a "desk"—actually a long table where manual typewriters were lined up and manned (and, yes, it was a largely male world) by people whose job it was to take down dictated stories or to actually write stories that were told to them on the spot by reporters in the field. Calls would come in, you'd slap your headphones on, and then go to work taking down what was often jumbled, on-the-spot coverage of some event happening a world away.

In the middle of the night my phone jingled. I was the only one on the desk that time since it was a slow news cycle and on the other end was a guy named Solomon Steckel calling from Israel. In the background, I heard what sounded like mortar fire and gunshots. He was calling from a phone booth in the middle of a firefight in what turned out to be the start of the Six-Day War. Wow! This was a huge story and a real scoop for our paper. I looked around, thinking I needed to hand this story over to someone with experience, but there was no one in the newsroom but me. Solomon told me he was lying on the floor of the phone booth to avoid getting shot!

I felt like I was in one of those 1930s movies about girl reporters! I gritted my teeth and began to type furiously. Over the next few minutes Solomon shouted his story to the rapid cadence of gunfire, and I took it down. Suddenly the line went dead. I didn't have time to ask him to repeat or refine anything. I looked at what I had typed, and it was a little scattered so I did my job and cleaned up the story.

When the night editor returned, he was flabbergasted, excited, and amazed that I'd been able to do all that. The story I "rewrote" made the front page that morning in a banner headline, and it had Solomon Steckel's byline, but I took the "special to the Star" tag as a special salute to me. So whose story was it really? Solomon's or mine because I'd altered it? I kept to the facts and kept to his exact expressions most of the time, but nevertheless I had "filtered" it. Did I feel dishonest or that I was spinning the news? Not at all. But keep in mind that it was still a rewrite and that kind of thing happens to news all over the world.

Is it different now that reporters are embedded with our fighting troops? Not really. Take the story Chris Kyle tells in his book (now a movie) *American Sniper*. He writes,

> *You'd be crucified if you didn't strictly obey the ROEs (Rules of Engagement). Back in Fallujah, there was an incident involving Marines clearing a house. A unit had gone into a house, stepping over some bodies as they moved to clear the rooms. Unfortunately, one of the bastards on the ground wasn't dead. After the marines were in the house, he rolled over and pulled the pin on a grenade. It exploded killing or wounding some of the Marines.*

> *From then on, the Marines started putting a round in anybody they saw as they entered a house. At some point, a newsman with a camera recorded this; the video became public and the Marines got in trouble. Charges were either dropped or never actually filed, since the initial investigation explained the circumstances. Still, even the potential for charges was something you were always aware of. The worst thing that you could ever do for that war was having all those media people embedded in the units.*
>
> (Kyle, 2012, pp. 298–299)

Even with embedding, we still don't get the entire story. Reporting now has become an art because it includes just the right amount of spin to get the story across according to what your editors tell you to "see." How much truth is there in journalism? I'm sure that most journalists are ethical and try to tell an unbiased story, but things happen.

The point of my telling you this story has to do with the kinds of choices we make when we tell stories. We may be interested in a particular theme and then assume that we are delivering truth about that, but at its core, it's our own truth we're always telling. All movies start with a theme. Something you want to make a film about should be something that interests you deeply. If you think that only applies to documentaries, you'd be wrong. Every piece of art should be based on what the artist wants and needs to say about life and the human condition.

Compromise is usually involved. That's because certain influences seep in that sometimes force us to contort or augment our truth slightly. For example, if we're funded by certain organizations, we might be asked to tweak things that emphasize its particular interest. Now, of course, this implies that you're totally on board with an organization before you take its money, but still there are certain artistic subtleties that you might have to forfeit in order to get your project made.

That means you need to know where to draw the line at compromise. Make sure there are waters in which you will not swim! Know this beforehand and stand firm. You need to have principles that keep you true to yourself. If you neglect these in order to get your film made, you'll eventually end up hating yourself. As Tolstoy says,

> *All compromise with institutions of which your conscience disapproves—compromises which are usually made for the sake of the general good—instead of producing the good you expected, inevitably lead you not only to acknowledge the institution you disapprove of, but also to participate in the evil that institution produces.*
>
> (Tolstoy, 2005, p. xvi)

Applying this practically may mean several things. For example, "institutions" and general good can mean studios, audiences, and the marketplace. If you are urged to include more violence than you'd normally approve of or more graphic sex or even more reliance on certain conventions, for example, you are advocating that particular construct. Make sure that you are on board with that because, if not, you'll have an impossible time explaining yourself. I've seen lots of filmmakers get up in front of audiences and try to justify images in their films that they don't particularly believe in. Pretty embarrassing and hard to watch.

I write about that in the introduction to my book *Screenwriting with a Conscience: Ethics for Screenwriters*. (2004, p. 8):

> *I believe each one of us knows when we are being honest and what is just and fair but sometimes, because of the stakes/rewards presented and the temptations that exist all around us, we give in and behave dishonestly, unjustly, unfairly—in short, unethically. It's this giving in that we've got to fight and the only way*

in which we can fight it is to be aware of our own personal code of ethics and make a strong personal commitment to it.

You need to define your code, and you've got to put it in practice in your work. You've got to stand behind your work because your work represents you! That means you've got to write about things that matter to you . . . themes you find compelling on a personal level. Knowing this makes choosing an engaging story audiences will spark to amazingly simple. All you have to do is find the story in which you are personally involved at some level. That doesn't mean the story has to be about your own life or experience, but it must have a theme that you resonate with because of something in your own life and/or psyche. And to feel that emotional resonance, you must be able to connect it to your own emotional core.

So we're back to my student who had trouble choosing. And that's because he couldn't relate to his own emotional core—the point at which he actually became emotionally involved with his story. Intellectual involvement won't do it. In fact, it will mess us up because our minds can come up with myriad excuses and reasons why something will or won't work. The mind has to be set aside (Biff Rose sang a song called "Forget Your Mind and You'll be Free"), and that's the tenet of all forms of meditation.

You've got to be still enough to get to your core, and sometimes when you do that it means making decisions that might seem crazy intellectually though right internally. We've got to listen to our guts and be able to choose stories that mean a lot to us on a myriad of levels.

Exercise

Write a list of themes that interest you.

Examples:

- Love
- Honor
- Financial gain
- Dishonesty
- Corporate greed
- Betrayal
- Infidelity

Now write down an image from your own life that you immediately associate with that theme—an image that makes that theme personal and real to you. Remembering an image of the first time you developed an interest in that theme is a good start.

For example, one of my students in his theme list came up with anger. His image had to do with a time when he was arguing with his mother about what college he should go to. The argument escalated. Out of that theme—a son wanting to be independent from the mother who raised him, wanting to assert himself as a man while she still thought of him as a boy—gave rise to a mother–son story where the son tries to gain independence in ways that are not always productive. And the student didn't come into the course knowing what he was going to write about.

This exercise works exceptionally well in helping you discover stories and images that resonate with you and because they do, will resonate with audiences. But let's say you have a theme but no story to attack it with. For example, one of my students knew he wanted to write a story about his grandfather who grew up in an orphanage run by a cruel person and escaped from that orphanage to live a wonderful life. He didn't know where to start because there were so many aspects to the story. I had him do the following exercise.

Ten-Second Image Blurt Exercise

Without thinking and in no more than about 10 seconds write down as many images as you "see" connected to your story. Don't dwell on these images or ask yourself if they are appropriate. Just think of your story and then conjure up images one after the other. Let your mind do the work!

My student's list looked like this:

> Train trestle
> Shabby room
> Hill at night under stars
> Broken window
> Two kids holding hands

A great list . . . because if you use these images, you can come up with a starting place for the movie, and because he didn't know where to start, this gave him a push. For example, the film could start with the sound of a train. In a shabby room, in a dark night, a boy sits by a broken window and looks out to watch the train going over a nearby trestle. He puts on his coat and sneaks out of his room. He's soon sitting on a hill looking up at a sky full of stars. Suddenly someone sits down beside him. It's a girl about his age, wearing a brightly colored old-fashioned cape. She reaches out and takes the boy's hand. They huddle together.

You can see how these images put together can give you an opening that creates interest and gives rise to interesting questions. Who's the boy? Why is his room shabby? Why does he have to sneak out? How did he get there? Why does he stop at the hill? Why doesn't he try to get to the train? Who is the girl? Where did she get that cape? What is her connection to the boy?

These images and the questions they raised gave my student a way into his film and helped him develop his story.

Sometimes we really need to find a way into the film, and even though the images may not necessarily come from the beginning of the story, they can at least suggest avenues of attack. In my student's case, the train trestle image wasn't used until the end of his film but helped him build the desire for escape in his characters and provided a goal for them to work toward.

Character Blast Exercise

You can do the same thing for character that you did with images. Because all stories come from characters, you may be able to get a story idea based on a character you visualize strongly. Here's how to do that.

1. Close your eyes and describe a character that pops into your head. (I came up with a grizzled gnome sitting on a stump.)
2. Go with that image and describe the character physically. (My gnome is wearing jodhpurs, a green hat, a red waistcoat, and blue shoes and carrying a broom.)
3. Now decide what that character is doing there. (My gnome is a stable hand charged with stall cleaning and is taking a break to munch on a small tea cake.)
4. Have your character engage in an activity, the first that comes to mind. (The gnome finishes eating, gets up, goes to the stable block, and starts sweeping a stall in which a giant white horse is in residence.)
5. Interrupt your character's action by an event. (Suddenly, a beautiful girl appears wearing a silver jumpsuit and carrying a saddle. She saddles the large horse and starts to take him out of the stall.)
6. Have the character react to the event. (The gnome grabs the horse's bridle and refuses to let go. He will not allow the horse to leave the stable.)

7. Describe the consequences of the character's action. (The girl snarls, grabs the gnome, and tries to toss him aside but he waves his wrist and turns the girl into a pussy cat, which he picks up and gently puts out of the stable. He locks the door and finishes sweeping.)
8. Give us a wild finish. (When he's done, the gnome snaps his fingers, turns himself into a handsome prince, fetches the pussy cat, and turns her back into the beautiful girl. He takes her in his arms and they embrace wildly. When they stop kissing she says, "Enough role playing for one day!")

Character conjuring has given us a little story (albeit absurd) that we can play with and make into a short film. If you follow the character, the actions that character takes will lead you into a series of events you can mold into something useful.

Sometimes, these image blasts can give you an entire first act, a second act, or even the entire short. Your challenge is to work toward making them significant in your story development. And as you're developing your story, you need to decide whether your story works better as a short or a feature.

Certain ideas lend themselves better to features. For example, stories with significant subplots that explain, augment, or essentially enrich the central plot are more feature specific. That's also true for some sci-fi stories that require an elaborate world setup. That doesn't mean that you can't do sci-fi shorts. It just takes some really clever world setup and a simpler approach. If your world is intensely complicated, you should probably turn your idea into a feature.

Stories that can be told simply, need little or no augmentation or subplot, are powerful in their own right, have no need of extraneous characters or multiple locations, and can be related with a great amount of energy from beginning to end make great shorts. That doesn't mean that all your stories have to be quick paced or "high concept." You can write a fabulous short that is atmospheric, poetic, or slow paced. You just need to make sure that your short can stand alone and has a beginning, middle, and end (even if that end is ambiguous).

In another chapter we'll talk about how you can write a short based on a feature, but now we'll look at shorts as a starting point in your career.

References

Beker, Marilyn. *Screenwriting with a Conscience: Ethics for Screenwriters.* Mahwah, NJ: Lawrence Erlbaum, 2004.
Kyle, Chris. *American Sniper.* New York: William Morrow, 2012.
Tolstoy, Leo. *What Is Art?* New York: Barnes and Noble, 2005.

3

THE SHORT ANSWER

As I mentioned in the introduction, there are lots of reasons to write and make a short film. Perhaps the most obvious reason is to gain access to audiences. It's much easier to get lots of people to see your short—particularly if you post it online in open forums like Vimeo or YouTube. We'll talk more about venues later.

A short film is a great calling card that can showcase your talent to lots of people who don't have long attention spans, and sadly, that's most of us. We're all movement junkies. As a culture we have trouble keeping still. We're always looking for the next thing—for newer sights and sounds. We're always looking for stimulation, and this search for constant jolts drives us to do "unnatural things," like checking our smart phones every few minutes and gorging on YouTube videos.

Canadian columnist McLen Greaves writing in *Zoomer Magazine,* July 2015 tells us that according to Statistic Brin Research Institute, our average attention span has dropped from 12 seconds in 2000 to an anorexic 8 seconds in 2013. The average attention span of a goldfish in comparison is 9 seconds.

He reported that college age kids now own an average of 6.9 devices and have subconsciously responded to information overload with speed. Facebook research shows that updates are getting shorter (Twitter has a 140-character limit) and sending email has been leapfrogged by messaging apps like WhatsApp, KIK, Messenger, and Line. And young Internet users are often foregoing words for pictures, fueling the rise of photo-sharing messaging apps like Instagram, Snapchat, and the Twitter-owned Vine where videos are limited to six seconds!

The bad news is that this creates some major problems in the way we all think, particularly in those with what I call "jolt addiction." Greaves (2014; p. 30) writes that

> *a China-based research team ran MRI scans on 18 college age students who fit the description of Internet addicts. Results showed several parts of the addicts' brains had shrunk up to 20 per cent including parts of the brain tied into Executive Function Disorder—a kind of new ADHD diagnosis flagged by teachers, parents and counselors as an inability to create and finish a plan.*

Pretty daunting!

Those of us interested in reaching vast audiences to relay our messages are forced to vie for attention in this jolt-seeking world—a vast and glowing market that demands continuous entertainment. But given the speed at which people tend to like moving, that entertainment has got to be short, quick, and easy. As I already mentioned, a variety of platforms have been designed specifically to satisfy that addiction. Facebook, YouTube, Twitter, Instagram, Tumblr, etc., all deal with the explosion of images and fast facts, the sharing of media jolts, that document lives and ideas.

Years ago, Marshall McLuhan defined and predicted "Blip Culture." He was talking about the way people like to get their news. He predicted the obsolescence of print and the dependence on electronic media and described how we'll all increasingly get our information in sound bites. But wait—what about an art form like film?

Unfortunately those who have been raised on film as a traditional art form are discovering that film has taken on a new meaning and direction. Film is more disposable and quick. Certainly, it's more efficient, and it's not even "film" any more but a series of pixels—pointillism gone wild—entirely digital and extraordinarily popular.

Independent filmmakers are realizing they no longer need be bound by the idea that movies must be long and expensive. In fact, the current marketplace eschews long and yearns for short.

Even in the industry, people aren't wild about reading 120 pages. Spec scripts aren't selling well and have to go through an intense vetting gauntlet just to get the "right" people to read them. And even then, they're often not read. If you want someone to get a glimpse of your work, there's no better way than to send that person a 5- to 7-minute short that demonstrates what you can do with story. That short can also demonstrate your sensibility and how you approach dialogue. That means you'll have to make sure that the short you write is produced well with great actors and good production quality.

In my interview with Marshall Nord of Shorts HD, he said he'd

> *had meetings lately with some other companies like Ron Howard and Brian Grazer. They started this digital incubator company with Discovery and they are saying oh we're going to make digital short form movies. They are doing 10 short form films. What they are doing is what I was doing when I was an executive at Dreamworks. They are going out and pitching their projects and it used to be show me a pilot or some tape and now what it has turned into is "show me the short form."*

Nord goes on to say that he

> *used to think that a good short film had a twist to it . . . like a Hitchcockian thing but that's too formula. I would say a clear concise idea told and executed well and what short film*

allows you to do is not be constrained to any formulaic structure. They say television and film is a collaborative medium and everyone puts their scent on it but in short film if you are an auteur. It really is your project whereas if you get paid or if you're writing for a particular purpose you have to craft it in a certain way.

That, of course, doesn't mean that shorts have no structure to them. They very much do, but the structure is simple and doesn't have the very particular structure confines of a feature. The short film mirrors the structure of a feature without the subplot and the spikes that propel plot points. We'll see how this works in a later chapter when we break down a feature and reimagine it into a new-entity short film. But for now, know that as long as your short film has a beginning, middle, and end (three acts essentially), it can be as loose or as "experimental" as you choose to make it.

Keep in mind though that if your goal is to eventually make commercial features (and by that I mean films that can be distributed for larger audiences), your short films shouldn't be so freeform experimental as to turn audiences, distributors, and investors off. You want to make people believe in your vision and your story-telling ability in a marketplace that is highly demanding on all levels. And there are lots of opportunities to make money and showcase your talents at the same time by making short films for that marketplace. For example, on April 10, 2015, *The Los Angeles Times* featured a front page Business Section story describing how JW Marriott hopes its short movies will draw younger travelers.

Marriott not only starred in the film (the first of several it plans to make) but also took the unusual step of producing "Two Bellmen" (a 17 minute film about two bellhops who thwart an art heist) at a cost of about $200,000. Since the *film was distributed on YouTube May, 2014 it has attracted more than 5 million views (to April, 2015).*

It's the first of several short films the world's largest hotel chain is producing to help promote its brand to a younger generation of travelers. Marriott "has launched its own studio to make short films showcasing its diverse properties which span 4, 100 hotel properties representing 19 brands in 76 countries. Driving Marriott's foray into entertainment are fundamental shifts in the advertising market. As millennials shun traditional ads and spend more time on YouTube and other digital platforms, hotels are having to rethink the ways they market their brands to younger travelers.
(*Los Angeles Times*, 2015, p. 1C)

Other companies and institutions are jumping on this very lucrative (for filmmakers) bandwagon broadening the possibilities for new filmmakers to get their work seen and earn some money doing that. Because of the explosion of new platforms, it's possible to actually get a job making films that doesn't involve beating down the doors of impregnable studios or production companies. That means having a short film as a sample of what you can do is a powerful tool that trumps any resume.

This kind of magic happened to one of my students, Gregory Hansen, back in 1993. He wrote and directed a short called *7 Souls*, and it was so good it got snapped up and made into a feature called *Heart and Souls* starring Robert Downey, Jr. Greg got to write the script, and this launched him on a screenwriting career. Many now famous directors started their careers making short film or industrials or music videos.

Noah Pisner (July 2015), writing on the site Arts.Mic, put forward 16 short films that launched the careers of famous directors. Here's some of what he had to say about several of them.

- **Benh Zeitlin,** *Glory at Sea* **(2008)**
  In 2012, Zeitlin's debut feature *Beasts of the Southern Wild* swept the festival circuit, winning top prizes at both the Sundance and Cannes film festivals before ultimately picking up four Oscar nominations. Funding for the film wouldn't have been possible, however, had Zeitlin not won an award at South by Southwest in 2008 with the premiere of his precursor short, *Glory at Sea*. Rendered in post–Hurricane Katrina grief with an overwhelming sense of magic realism, the short offers a much tighter encapsulation of *Beasts*, but with equally epic aspirations.
- **Michel Gondry,** *Human Behavior* **(1993)**
  Gondry—like Spike Jonze and David Fincher—entered into feature film making via music video production. In 1993, the style of Gondry's early videos for his own band Oui Oui caught the attention of Björk, who asked him to direct a video for her song "Human Behavior." In the production, Gondry shows off his trademark style: a stop-animation-esque approach depicting dreamlike mechanizations and the glitchy imagery of soaring meteors.

  The neosurrealist aesthetic catapulted Gondry into the top tier of music video auteurs, setting him off producing videos for the likes of Radiohead and Beck before bringing him to the attention of screenwriter Charlie Kaufman, whom he would go on to collaborate with on his first two feature films, *Human Nature* and *Eternal Sunshine of the Spotless Mind*.

  The one other short that was essential to Gondry's rise to fame was his Levi's 501 "Drugstore" commercial back in 1996. According to the Guinness World Records 2004, this spot holds the distinction for "Most Awards Won by a TV Commercial."

- **Sophia Coppola** *Lick the Star* **(1998)**
  Coppola wrote and directed *Lick the Star*, a 14-minute film that premiered on the Independent Film Channel. The film shows the beginnings of Coppola's unique cinematic style: Sharp cutting, stark compositions and rock 'n' roll music all help frame the downfall of the most popular girl in high school. The film prefigures themes and images of many of Coppola's later works. The opening scene shows the lead actress being driven in a car—a running trope that has remained in almost every single opening scene in her features since: *The Virgin Suicides, Lost in Translation* and *Somewhere*.

- **Jared Hess,** *Peluca* **(2003)**
  Before Jon Heder played the titular character in 2004's breakout indie hit *Napoleon Dynamite*, the actor starred as the same character (only going by the name of Seth) in director Hess' student short film *Peluca*. The short was made for only $500 on black-and-white 16-mm film stock in Hess' hometown of Preston, Idaho, over the course of two days. After being shown during the Slamdance Film Festival in 2003, Hess was encouraged by a producer to adapt the short into a low-budget feature. *Napoleon Dynamite* came out the following year, enabling Hess' rise as an indie director and Heder's rise as a comedy star.

- **Gary Gray,** *"It Was a Good Day"* **(1993)**
  Gray was relatively unknown when Ice Cube hired him to make the video [for "It Was a Good Day"]. Its success then prompted the rapper to ask Gray to direct the film he was co-writing. Made for only $2 million, *Friday*, starring Ice Cube and Chris Tucker, grossed $30 million, paving the way for several sequels. Over the next decade, Gray proved his versatility with films like *The Negotiator* and *The Italian Job*. Recently, it was

announced that he had beaten out John Singleton (*Boyz n the Hood*) and George Tillman Jr. (*Notorious*) for the chance to direct the 2015 NWA biopic, *Straight Outta Compton*, with Ice Cube, nominated for best screenplay at the 2016 Academy Awards.

- **Paul Thomas Anderson, *Cigarettes & Coffee* (1993)**
  The critically adored director of *There Will Be Blood* and *The Master* owes his career to a big break at Sundance in 1993. Anderson spent his college fund and some gambling winnings to make the short, *Cigarettes & Coffee*, which tells the story of five people all interconnected through a $20 bill. On the strength of the short, Anderson was then invited to the Sundance filmmakers lab, where he worked on adapting the short into a feature. The film became *Hard Eight*, which premiered at Cannes in 1996, launching one of the most important cinematic careers of the past few decades.

- **Tim Burton, *Frankenweenie* (1984)**
  In 2007, Disney signed Burton to direct a stop-motion animated remake of Burton's own 1984 short film *Frankenweenie*. Right out of CalArts, Disney commissioned Burton to make the original live-action short to precede the 1984 re-release of *Pinocchio* in theaters. The film's bleak tone didn't meet the studio's expectations for a family film, however, so Disney decided to shelve the project and fire Burton. Luckily, around the same time, Paul Reubens was looking for a director for a film idea he had been developing. Stephen King had seen Burton's short, and strongly recommended it to Reubens. Reubens arranged to meet with Burton and offered him his breakout opportunity, directing *Pee-Wee's Big Adventure*. The full-length animated version of *Frankenweenie* was released in 2012 and received nominations for an Academy Award for Best Animated Feature Film.

- **Wes Anderson, *Bottle Rocket* (1994)**
  Anderson's original 1994 black and white version of *Bottle Rocket* has likely done more to launch its director's career than any other short film ever. The making of the film has almost become apocryphal: In 1992 Anderson and Owen Wilson met in a playwriting class [at] UT Austin. The two wrote a script together, which followed the exploits of three clueless would-be criminals, who would be played by Robert Musgrave, Wilson and his brother, Luke. During the 1994 Sundance Film Festival, *Bottle Rocket* received little attention from critics and attendees, but managed to catch the eye of producer James Brooks, who funded the duo's debut feature based on the short.

  The difference between the 13-minute short and the 92-minute feature are mostly cosmetic—the narrative was expanded, and color photography was used. The feature also ditched the short's jazzy soundtrack for a new score from former Devo member Mark Mothersbaugh. Upon release, the feature quickly gained cult status among critics and cinephiles. Martin Scorsese named the film one of his 10 favorite movies of the decade. The accolade prompted Disney to finance Wilson and Anderson's next film project, *Rushmore*, which ushered in a cast of recurrent collaborators—Bill Murray, most notably—who have ardently worked to help Anderson make many of the films that have defined modern cinema: *The Royal Tenenbaums, Fantastic Mr. Fox, Moonrise Kingdom.* And most recently *The Grand Budapest Hotel* that in 2015 won 4 Oscars with another 141 wins and 153 nominations." (Pisner, 2015)

If you go to the Art.Mic site you can see these films and the others that Posner names. These are only a few in the vast pantheon of shorts that launched careers and even Oscars. (Think *Whiplash*, the short made in 2013 that two years later ended up as an Academy Award–nominated feature!)

So now that you've seen how short films can help you move your career along and even make you money, you're ready to think about how to craft your story to make it into a powerful short.

References

Bottle Rocket. Dir. Wes Anderson. 1994. Short film.
Cigarettes & Coffee. Dir. Thomas Anderson. 1993. Short film.
Frankenweenie. Dir. Tim Burton. 1984. Short film.
Glory at Sea. Dir. Benh Zeitlin. 2008. Short film.
Greaves, McLen. 10 Reasons Why Almost All Internet Articles Are Lists. *Zoomer Magazine*, September 2014, p. 30.
Human Behavior. Dir. Michel Gondry. 1993. Short film.
It Was a Good Day. Dir. Gary Gray. 1993. Short film.
Lick the Star. Dir. Sophia Coppola. 1998. Short film.
Marriott, J. W. Room for Films. *Los Angeles Times*, Friday, April 10, 2015, p. 1 C.
Peluca. Dir. Jared Hess. 2003. Short film.
Pisner, Noah. *16 Short Films that Launched the Careers of Famous Directors*, Arts.mic, July 15, 2014, *https://mic.com/articles/92951/16-short-films-that-launched-the-careers-of-famous-directors#.xD1jOJBUK*. Accessed 18 November 2016.

4

THE SHORT BIBLE

1. Keep It Short

How short (or long) should a short film be? Back in the day, when I wrote my first short, the going length was 30 minutes. Festivals and distributors were more tolerant of that length and in fact wanted to see it. However, now with platforms tight for space and in the thick of Blip Culture (as McLuhan predicted) shorts really do need to be short.

Depending on the platform for which your short is intended, it can be anywhere from 2 to 15 minutes. And 15 minutes is pushing the outside time edge. That's because if you want your short to play in festivals, it shouldn't go over 15 minutes. Festival programmers are especially cramped for space and won't slot anything longer than 15 minutes. In fact, the optimum time for a short film is 12 minutes.

Festival programmer and consultant Thomas Ethan Harris (we'll hear more from him later) says most festivals like Sundance program 7 to 10 shorts per program and if your film crosses the 15-minute mark, it won't play at many festivals. That's not good because you want as many opportunities to show your film as possible. We'll get more into the festival scene in a later chapter. Right now, though, know that it's essential that your short be festival friendly, and that starts with making it no longer than 15 minutes.

This kind of finagling requires that you develop your story carefully by outlining it first and making sure you've thought through all the possibilities. Because you need to tell the story as quickly and efficiently as you can but still give a lot of bang for the buck, your storytelling needs to be tight and powerful. You can get that figured out when you outline to length. And keep in mind, if you do write something to length you won't have the heartache and sometimes impossible task of taking things out.

My students always argue that they can't possibly say what they want to say in that amount of time, but by the time we're through developing, outlining, and writing the script, they see that it's possible and usually perfect for impact and execution. In fact, they often find they can do what they want in less than 15 minutes.

That's because writers often spend too much time writing scenes that are unnecessary, redundant, or repetitive. The usual culprit is dialogue, which often runs way longer than it needs to. [We'll deal with that in a subsequent "should."] Too much time is spent introducing characters. Too much time is spent on exposition. All of these pitfalls can be avoided if the writer concentrates on telling the story in the most visual way possible.

Keep in mind that audiences are very sophisticated these days. They are used to getting information in small increments. That means you don't need to explain as much or be as obvious. In the old days (the great classic movies of yore) audiences were willing to sit still for expanded dialogue-heavy scenes with intricate exposition. Not today. Get it out and get it done! You'd be surprised what you can do in even two minutes if you are ruthless with yourself. Case in point—that Levi's movie by Michel Gondry. But that doesn't mean your film has to be paced like a commercial. There are other options that can work just as well.

2. Pace Yourself

The pace of your film is extremely important. Audiences need to be introduced to that pace in the first act. In a feature, you can write a rather slow first act and then pick up the pace gradually. In a short, you don't have time to do that so you need to be pretty sure about the pace early on. That means establishing the mood right away visually and, if you need to, through dialogue. The pace you set up determines how the film will be shot. So if you are taking a long leisurely time describing things, you are indicating that the camera movements need to mirror that leisure. But remember, just because a film is slow paced, it doesn't mean that it has to be boring, long, or tedious. Think of it as a seduction. You want the audience to be intrigued and interested right away. It's a kind of flirt until the actual clothes ripping off at the end of the first act.

Naturally, if you are writing an action piece or a mystery or some other kind of film that lends itself to showing what it's got right away, you have to do that. Make sure that the audience thrills to an action scene or is mystified very quickly. The same is true for comedy. Make sure that you get laughs as soon as possible. No time to dawdle here. Remember that people looking at your film see a lot of what they call "product" so if they aren't interested, intrigued, captivated, or mesmerized in the first few minutes, you've lost them.

3. Stay on Structure

This pacing issue dovetails with structure. As I mentioned earlier, shorts do have a specific structure—beginning, middle, end. That means they have three acts. As in all movies, act one establishes the genre, presents atmosphere, introduces characters, and puts forward the main "problem" or defining situation of the movie we're about to see. In features, the first act usually runs about 30 minutes, ending around page 28 to 32 of the screenplay. That's because you've got 120 pages to work with and you can take your time doing everything you need to establish the characters and the story. Act two, running from pages 30 to 90, unfolds the story with subplots and twists. Act three, where everything is resolved, begins at page 90 and can end anywhere (100 to 110) to page 120. The third act can be quick and short.

In order to make this perfectly clear here's how a feature is outlined to structure using plot points. A plot point is something that moves the action forward about every five movie minutes. It can be one scene or even two or three short scenes. Using the fact that one minute of screen time roughly equals one page of script, one plot point will take about five pages.

In the writing of the movie, you may find that some points take fewer pages and some more, but as a rule, the general page count is five pages a plot point. That means in a two-hour movie, you've got 24 plot points to tell your story.

The following outline template organizes the plot points in a two-hour movie into a format that's structure perfect.

Full-Length Screenplay 24-Point Outline

ACT ONE *(Goal: To Establish Genre, Characters, Atmosphere, Problem)*

1.
2. *(Page 10 hook)*
3. *(Page 15 inciting incident)*
4.
5.
6. **END OF ACT ONE (p. 30)**

ACT TWO *(Goal: To Further Develop Characters, Working on Solving the Problem with Twists)*

7.

8.
9. **Second Act SPIKE #1 (p. 45)** *(substantial movement in early Act Two to propel attention)*
10.
11.
12. **MIDPOINT (p. 60)** *(The middle of the movie. Major move forward.)*
13.
14.
15. **Second Act SPIKE #2 (p. 75)** *(Substantial movement to propel to end of act)*
16.
17.
18. **END OF ACT TWO (p. 90)** *(Move toward Resolution and tie-up)*

ACT THREE *(Goal: To Solve the Problem, Tie Up Relationships, Bring Home Issues)*

19. **BEGINNING OF ACT THREE.**
20.
21.
22.
23.
24.

When you're filling in the outline, you may not know all the plot points, but you should definitely figure out the major points, that is, plot point 6 (End of Act One–page 30), plot point 9 (Spike #1 in Act Two—page 45), plot point 12 (Midpoint—page 60), plot point 15 (Spike S#2 in Act Two—page 75), and plot point 18 (the end of Act Two—page 90).

You may know plot points 1, 2, and 3 but not 4 and 5, and then you may know 6 but not 7 and 8. The plot points you leave blank are where you can slot in your subplot.

Short sentences are used to create the outline. Scenes may be included in point form under the defining sentence of the point. For example:

1. John and Alfreda meet when John walks his pet dragon into Starbucks.

    - They become entangled in the dragon's leash.
    - The dragon escapes as Alfreda faints (she's terrified of reptiles).
    - John kisses her passionately. It's love at first sight and to hell with the dragon!

In a 90-minute movie, the template will vary slightly, still keeping to structure: Act One will end at about page 20 to 23, the first spike in Act Two will be on page 35, the midpoint will be at page 45, the second spike will be at page 60, and the end of Act Two will be at page 75. Act Three goes from pages 75 to 90. If the movie extends past two hours (not a good idea these days—studios hate that!) the plot points will change accordingly to make the second act longer—sometimes by adding a third spike—and will make the third act longer too.

Short films are structured the same way but with different page counts and without the spikes, because programmable shorts run anywhere from 5 to 15 minutes so there is no time for subplots. The act breaks in a short behave as spikes to move the action forward, although there can be small spikes throughout the second act of a 15-minute short. That's not something to be concerned about. This will happen naturally with the flow of the story.

The first thing to do is write a paragraph synopsis of your story. Then outline your story in point form. Take a look at the outline. If it runs ultra-long and doesn't fit into a preferred short length, you will need to trim as necessary. Think carefully about each plot point to determine if it's really necessary to tell your story. Remember that extra or extraneous scenes to make a point already obvious will cost you money and precious time. Be ruthless and tough. This outline needs to be a lean machine to produce a lean and tight short film.

Keep in mind that you're going to outline and write to structure. I'm a great proponent of writing to length and structure. If you don't do that, you'll end up with a first draft that is ungainly and difficult, if not impossible, to trim. (We all hate destroying our bon mots!)

Your outline should look like one of the outlines I've modeled here. Again, keep the outline short and in point form so you can play with it. It's important to remember in all models that the first act of a short film is crucial and must be quick and powerful, drawing audiences into the film as soon as possible. Act One should be relatively short. And you might not need a lot of pages for a quick resolution in Act Three. You can play with that too if you need to give your Act Two more weight.

Model One: Fifteen-Minute Movie

Act One: pages 1 to 5
Act Two: pages 6 to 12
Act Three: pages 13 to 15

Model Two: Five-Minute Movie

Act One: page 1
Act Two: pages 2 to 4
Act Three: page 5

Model 3: Seven-Minute Movie

Act One: pages 1 to 2
Act Two: pages 3 to 6
Act Three: page 7
In this one you can make Act Two shorter if you want and make your Act Three two pages.

Model 4: Ten-Minute Movie

Act One: pages 1 to 3
Act Two: pages 4 to 8
Act Three: pages 9 to 10

If you want to make Act Two a little longer, you can extend it to page 9 and do a quick resolving Act Three in one page.

You get the idea. You can adapt the models to 12 minutes or any other programmable length.

As I explained earlier, the key is getting into your story as early, efficiently, and as quickly as possible. In features, that's done by creating a 10-page hook (as the outline template shows) that will grab the audience within the first 10 minutes of the film. In shorts, the first act is really the hook and it's got to be powerful, direct, and elegant. Audiences shouldn't even be aware that they've been grabbed by the eyeballs and can't look away. They're just simply along for the ride from the gate.

Here's an example of how to outline the same story for different lengths using a sample paragraph synopsis.

Synopsis:

> A man and a woman show up at the same bank at the same time intending to rob it. After an altercation they decide to team up. They do the job and leave in the guy's getaway car where the guy's partners are waiting for him. Turns out they're part of a much wanted robbery ring. The girl gets into a relationship with the guy, but he wants to do another big job. She's torn about this. She tells him she wants to go straight and tries to persuade him to do the same. He refuses. Right before they pull the job, she pulls out a couple of handcuffs and then her ID. She's an undercover cop and she busts him. But

wait . . . he starts laughing and pulls out his ID. He's an undercover cop too. They've both been trying to bust up the same ring.

Okay. So now let's outline this rather simple story in a few ways.

Model One: 15-Minute Movie Outline

Act One:

Page 1: Man gets out of a car where three other unsavory guys are sitting. He pulls on a ski mask and walks over to a dumpster behind the bank and puts on a ski mask.

Page 2: A few minutes later a woman arrives on the back of a motor bike. She waves to the person driving off, walks to the other side of the dumpster, and puts on a mask. The guy doesn't see her.

Page 3: They bump into each other and argue about whose bank it is to rob.

Page 4: They decide to team up and pull the job.

Page 5: They pull the job. The girl gets in the guy's getaway car, meets two other gang members, and they take off.

Act Two:

Page 6: They arrive at the gang's hideout. Money is divided and dynamics revealed.

Page 7: Sleeping arrangements. Girl is thrown together with guy.

Page 8: After witty banter they sleep in separate beds.

Page 9: Gang plans another job using girl as integral part of plan.

Page 10: Girl and guy get closer. She tries to talk him out of job.

Page 11: He refuses and they fight.

Page 12:	They make up and go to bed together. She agrees to do the job.

Act Three:

Page 13:	They approach another bank and case it.
Page 14:	They put their masks on and begin to enter the bank when the girl pulls out ID and cuffs.
Page 15:	The guy pauses and also pulls out ID and cuffs. He's been working undercover too. They laugh, put their masks on, do the job anyway, and they take off with cash and handcuffs.

I twisted the ending. I could have chosen to give away that the girl was an undercover cop by revealing this fact in the second act and intercutting between the gang stuff and the girl talking to the cop shop. The only danger with that is that it might make the movie longer. But if I really wanted to do that, I could cut the gang stuff altogether. But that's not an option because I need the gang stuff to explain why she doesn't bust him right away. She's undercover to bust the entire gang and so goes along with him. In this case, I think the undercover surprise is best left to the third act.

Model 2: Five-Minute Movie Outline

Act One:

Page 1:	Girl and guy meet at dumpster and argue about whose job it is. They decide to team up.

Act Two:

Page 2:	They do the job and drive away in the guy's getaway car.
Page 3:	At the guy's hideout they meet the rest of the gang. Girl and guy flirt and get close.
Page 4:	Girl and guy have wild sex and she tries to convince him to go straight. He refuses.

Act Three

Page 5: They both go to the bank and cuffs are pulled out by both of them. Laughter, etc. Quick cuts as they both bust the gang or rob and take off.

Model 3: Seven-Minute Movie Outline

Act One:

Page 1: Guy and girl show up at dumpster behind bank separately and pull on ski masks. They notice each other and argue about whose bank job it is.

Page 2: Argument resolves when they decide to team up. They pull the job.

Act Two

Page 3: Girl gets in his getaway car and they drive off.

Page 4: They arrive at the guy's hideout and meet the rest of the robbery gang.

Page 5: They plan another job as girl and guy get romantic fast.

Page 6: She begs him to call off job and go straight. He refuses.

Act Three:

Page 7: They approach the bank in masks when the girl pulls out her ID and cuffs. He laughs and does the same.

I didn't include the crooked cop thing in this one although I could have just as easily done that. There would be enough time to show them pulling off the job in a quick cut and riding into the sunset over credits!

Model 4: Ten-Minute Movie Outline

Act One:

Page 1: Guy and girl show up separately at dumpster behind bank and pull on ski masks. They

	notice each other and argue about whose bank job this is.
Page 2:	Argument resolves when they decide to team up. They rob the bank.

In this case Act One is the same as in the seven-minute movie. Acts Two and Three are where you can take a little more time.

Act Two:

Page 3:	She gets in his getaway car and they drive off.
Page 4:	They arrive at gang headquarters and discover the gang is notorious and is planning more jobs.
Page 5:	Girl and guy start to flirt and it's obvious a relationship is forming.
Page 6:	Gang decides to use girl as integral part of a new plan for an even bigger job.
Page 7:	Girl and guy get it on and she tries to convince him to go straight because she wants to go straight too.
Page 8:	He makes an effort to get girl out of the job but the gang insists she do it. She agrees.

Act Three:

Page 9:	They approach an even bigger bank. Cuffs come out. Mutual laughs.
Page 10:	They pull the job and ride off into the sunset. Quick cut to both of them on a beach in Bali!

In this story, you can begin the bank job scene in page 2 and carry it over to page 2½ if you need to. The act break transitions over these pages and that's okay.

When you adapt this structure to a 12-minute movie or any other length, you just have to make each plot point something that moves the action forward in a page or page and a half. Be creative but keep in mind that you don't have time to go off on tangents or give characters' back stories. We'll demonstrate how to introduce characters quickly and visually in point five of The Short Bible.

4. Keep It Visual

You need to determine that your short film will be as visual as you can make it. I know that you think this is a no-brainer when it comes to writing a movie, but, believe me, it's the single most problematic aspect when it comes to screenwriting. That's because the involvement with telling the story sometimes overshadows the mechanics of how to tell it strictly through pictures and not words.

Our history of storytelling is very audible. Visual storytelling always did exist via painting, sculpture, architecture, and dance, but in the computer years it's really exploded. Storytellers have so many more tools available to them. Sometimes that means words go by the wayside. This isn't a good thing either. The talent of the screenwriter lies in being able to make words visual and, by doing that, facilitate the making of a film that is highly so.

The only way screenwriters can do that is by seeing the movie in their minds and describing what they see. I tell my students to do this all the time. It's no use being intellectual about writing a film. That just doesn't work. The trick is to let the movie unfold in your mind's eye and then simply describe it. If you do that, your screenplay will be highly visual.

That goes for writing dialogue too. You've got to be able to hear it in your head and speak it out loud before you write it down. If you don't do that, it won't be natural. More about this later.

When you do this visualization, you may notice that things don't always turn out as you planned them. That's because you are giving your characters and story a life with movement and that movement may take an interesting and unusual direction. Rewrite your outline and go with it.

You'll be glad you did. And the way you can use visuals most effectively right from the start is to give as much information as you can about the story, and especially the characters, in as visual a manner as you possibly can.

If you want to really push yourself you can try an experiment. See if you can write your story entirely without dialogue. I'm not advocating making a silent film, but I am pointing out that sometimes we don't need words to let the audience know what's going on. Try the following exercise.

Exercise

Come up with a scene in which your characters have an interaction that furthers the plot of your story. Write this scene entirely without dialogue. The goal is to make sure that we know exactly what is going on without having to use dialogue.

5. Control Your Visuals

The old Hollywood saw that screenwriters are a necessary evil, only necessary to throw the story together so that the director and his minions can conjure up the movie on their own terms, is still somewhat in vogue today. Screenwriters can buy into that by being vague when they create visuals. When they do that, directors feel free to usurp what's written on the page and morph the movie in their own way. Unfortunately, they can do this anytime they want, but screenwriters make it easier for them to do that, giving up the power of their own vision by being obtuse or imprecise.

To really make sure that our ideas get onto the screen, we've got to be as precise as possible when creating our scenes. That doesn't mean that we've got to overwrite our descriptions, but it does mean that we can't be so vague as to let others take over what the audience sees. It's important to remember this: *what you write is what you get!* For instance, in a film about a chef worried about losing his restaurant, beginning students usually write something like this:

INT. RESTAURANT KITCHEN – NIGHT

>A chef cooks a fresh dish in a commercial kitchen. He nervously drops things and looks to see if anyone noticed. When he thinks he's safe he grabs the handle of a pot on the stove and burns his hand. Now others notice.

Not good. Although this may seem like an adequate enough description to get the scene going, it actually leaves too much to chance regarding the exact visuals necessary to further the story. The writer has not owned his or her movie and failed to relay exactly how he or she saw the scene. Things are implied rather than described. In order to take control, the description should go like this:

INT. RESTAURANT KITCHEN – NIGHT

>TOM, 26, wearing a chef's uniform bursting at the seams, stands in front of a grimy state-of-the art stove cutting butter into a frying pan. Still holding the butter, he picks up a slice of bread but drops it on the floor. As he stoops to pick it up, he drops the butter, slips, falls, and hits his head on the oven door handle.
>
>He jumps to attention and looks around nervously at the apron-clad worker beside him who's cutting vegetables. The worker smiles to himself but quickly pulls a neutral face. Tom looks relieved and grabs the handle of the frying pan but SCREAMS and pulls his hand away as the worker beside him shakes his head.

Writing the scene like this, without writing actual angles, dictates the shot. We'll first see Tom in a medium shot by the stove. When he starts dropping things, the shot widens so we can see him stoop and hit his head. The moment he looks around, the shot widens even more to include the apron-clad worker. Then the shot cuts to the worker in perhaps a medium close-up and cuts back to Tom when he grabs the handle of the frying pan. As he screams and pulls his hand away, the shot could widen. Or the shot could go wide to include the worker when Tom grabs the handle and stay wide.

This doesn't mean that you have to determine angles as you write. But what it does demonstrate is that the way you write it indicates to the director how to set up the shots, and if that director is you, then you've done a lot of the work of creating your shot list as you write the script. This goes right back to visualizing your scenes carefully in terms of how you want to see them and adding detail to get control of your shots. We'll use this example later in Chapter 8 to demonstrate how this kind of writing makes compiling shot lists easier.

You may think that this takes too much time in a short script, but keep in mind that you aren't writing the script to cheat length. You are crafting a film that must be exquisite in its every detail and to do that you need to take great care with each visual you present. An accurate description will give you subtext you need in your film.

In the little chef scenario the details we provide are essential. We learn that the chef is overweight (his uniform is bursting at the seams), uses real butter to cook with instead of lard or commercial fat of some kind, is nervous on a continuum (he drops the knife and then the butter and then he hits his head), is concerned about how others see him (the reaction of the worker whose reaction is also important because it demonstrates that he realizes the chef doesn't want to be seen as vulnerable) and is preoccupied enough to hurt himself (he grabs the hot frying pan handle without thinking). His scream indicates pain. We need all of that to get the real flavor of what's going on internally as well as externally. This kind of writing makes your screenplay richer and your work directing much easier.

6. Quickly Clarify Characters

In a feature you've got lots of time to introduce your main character throughout your first act. You can give us lots of detail up until the page 10 hook but then you can expound. You don't have that luxury in a short film. You've got to let your audience know your main character and get interested in that character as fast as you can. This isn't that hard to do if you have your wits about you and use visual storytelling to transmit as much information as you can without action or dialogue. You can, of course, use action but you also need to make use of small gestures, wardrobe, and production design to get your character across quickly. If you do that, you won't have to create convoluted and elaborate scenarios or throw in hideous expository dialogue to get the job done.

In *The Big Lebowski* and the first *Pirates of The Caribbean: The Curse of The Black Pearl*, that was done beautifully. I know these are features with lots of time to develop characters, but in spite of that, so much was revealed in so little time that they're stellar examples of how you could use those techniques in your short. You should look at the openings of these movies before or after you read this.

The Big Lebowski

The opening is very Shakespearean in that it gives us 2 minutes and 33 seconds of voiceover describing the location of the movie and Lebowski, the main character, before we even see him. And when we do actually see him, it only takes *1 minute and 10 seconds* to tell us lots about him.

The first time we see Lebowski, he looks like a bum. His hair is long and shaggy, his beard is unkempt, he's wearing sunglasses and an open bathrobe over a t-shirt and boxers. He casually ambles into a deserted, brightly lit supermarket. Because it's deserted, we assume it's night time which make the sunglasses he's wearing even more of a statement. Could he be stoned? Light sensitive? Copping an attitude? Probably all of the above.

Already we've got a lot of information about him. His wardrobe tells us he's nocturnal, sloppy, doesn't care what people think of him, and is comfortable in his own skin. But we soon find out that he might indeed care about how he's perceived because when he walks in, he looks around.

He approaches the dairy case, picks up a carton of half-and-half, examines the expiration date, picks up another carton, and compares the two. A quick shot of the clerk, who looks bored and indifferent, indicates to us that she's used to his shenanigans and is nonplussed. He's done this before. He puts the original carton back and then, looking around again (he seems to want to check if he's being watched and so he does care about how he's perceived), opens the carton and sniffs the contents. He pauses and ponders. Here's someone who doesn't make quick decisions. A few minutes later we see flecks of half-and-half trapped in his moustache. Smelling wasn't enough. He's had to taste the half-and-half to make sure it was okay.

At this point I usually ask my students what all this stuff with the half-and-half indicates. Usually only the brightest will realize what that is. Take a moment and see if you can figure it out.

Here's the answer: it shows that he has serious trust issues. He doesn't trust the date, he doesn't trust his own nose, and so he's got to sample the stuff. Here's a guy who has to experience things to believe them.

Now we get to finances. He leans over the counter and writes a check for 69 cents. The fact that it's an uneven amount of change is quirky. The clerk is again unfazed. He's a guy who doesn't carry cash. And as he's writing the check, he looks up at then President Bush talking about Iraq. That shows that he's interested in world events to some extent and also that he's easily distracted. And that he does pay attention to his surroundings.

Remember, all of this took only *1 minute and 10 seconds* and no dialogue!

When we cut to his house exterior (it was night after all), he's carrying a bowling bag and trotting up to his door. Clearly he's in a hurry to get there. Maybe he does have some place to go.

As he opens the door, he senses something—another clue that he's aware of his surroundings.

And then he's mugged by a thug who pushes him into the bathroom and plunges his head into the toilet, spilling the half-and-half.

In the ensuing conversation, we learn that he takes ad-versity with good humor ("Where's the money Lebowski . . ." It's somewhere down there, let me take another look"). He's fearless and confident. He posits proof that he's single by indicating the absence of a wedding ring and that his toilet seat is up. And by the way, we notice that the toilet paper roll is empty. Here's a guy who isn't too fastidious. Or is he? He does complain when thug #2 urinates on the rug. There are some things he does care about in a random sort of way. And, of course, here's where he tells us what he likes to be called by everyone . . . The Dude . . . not Lebowski. His moniker and image are important to him. He puts his sunglasses back on and continues to make sardonic quips.

We've really learned a lot about the character so far, and remember, we're only 1 minute and 10 seconds into the actual movie. That's the kind of economy I'm talking about when I say it's important to introduce your characters quickly and efficiently. You don't need lots of pages to do that. This film, in fact, didn't even need the 2-minute, 33-second voice-over at the top to get us into the character. We were hooked the moment we met Lebowski, and it took a total of only *1 minute and 10 seconds* to do it.

*Pirates of the Caribbean: The Curse of
the Black Pearl*

We get the same kind of speedy character revelation in the first minute of the first *Pirates of the Caribbean* movie when we meet Jack Sparrow. That movie opens moving in to a medium close-up of Jack. We're not sure where he is but we can tell a lot about him by the way he looks: a braided beard, beads in his hair, a well-worn hat and coat, a leather strap slung over his shoulder. He looks kind of dreamy, as if he's lost in thought and the thoughts aren't exactly happy ones but he looks only mildly sad and pensive. This has all been transmitted by Depp's acting here.

That's why you'll need to get an actor who can transmit a lot of information using facial expressions and inner acting work. We'll talk more about that later.

A wind blows up, and Jack is distracted. He looks down and then grabs a rope tied to what is clearly the mast of a ship and swings down. He's athletic and familiar with this practice.

When he lands, it's not on the deck of a magnificent ship but in the hull of a miserable little boat that's quickly filling with water. Without hesitation, he grabs a bucket and bails. And then he's distracted again by the hanging corpses of three pirates. Even though the boat is in desperate danger of sinking if he doesn't keep bailing, he stops what he's doing to pay homage—an overblown kind of homage where he lifts his hat and waves. He's certainly showy about the way he does things.

We already know that he's a little bit of a fop and a little pretentious. His clothes are outrageous and his movements seem contrived and overblown. He clearly fancies himself as a kind of theatrical gentleman but because of his homage to the hung pirates, we know that he's a pirate too.

When he pulls into a busy port he again stands proudly on the mast looking out into space. He's confident and in command. And then we notice that the mast is barely at the water line since most of the boat is below the water. Unperturbed, just as the mast reaches the dock, Jack steps off onto it without even looking down. He's so sure of himself he doesn't have to take ordinary precautions. And besides, what will all the people on the dock think if he does? Here's another guy whose image is ultra-important to him. He's not ashamed of his pathetic boat or his circumstances.

We've been given lots of information in *1 minute and 5 seconds* and not a word of dialogue has been spoken.

Because this is a feature, we get a lot more information through dialogue and action in the next 8 minutes and 14 seconds of the film that brings us to the page 10 hook. We learn that Jack is in disguise, not adverse to bribing and stealing, great with words, likes making witty banter, and enjoys making fools of people who he later takes into his confidence. (The two men guarding the ship wind up intrigued by his stories.) We also see that he is brave (he jumps in and saves the girl) and experienced (knows to rip off her dress and corset) and fearless. This information builds on the first minute of the movie and elaborates on what we already have surmised. In a short we can also do this while getting directly into the action.

For example, if the short movie was about a pirate commandeering a ship, we could end with Jack making a fool of the two guards and making off with the ship. Or if it was about rescuing the girl, we could cut down the dialogue with the guards, have him board the ship, immediately save the girl, and then run off with her into the sunset. In any case, we could still know very early on who Jack is.

But in order to do all of this with our characters, we need to construct a character biography to let us know who we're dealing with. And to do that, *you* have to know who *you're* dealing with.

Writers get into trouble because they really don't know their characters well enough. And to do that it's important for writers to think deeply about psychology and, yes, their own inner lives. Because all stories are formed by the writer's psyche, it stands to reason that all the characters the writer creates are different versions of himself. The old hippie adage "you got to be it to see it" really rings true here. Unless the writer can feel deeply the inner workings of all the characters he creates, the story, which arises from character, will fall flat.

Knowing Your Characters

To really understand your characters, it's necessary to create character biographies that have substantial back stories—events that shaped who they have become before the start of the movie. Superficial character traits created as lists just don't cut it. For example, you may knock off point-form character facts (appearance, height, birthplace, parents, etc.), but that list won't help you when it comes to writing situations in which your characters have to react. Rather, it's essential to write the backstory as a short story and include in that story things that you could use (even obliquely) later on in your screenplay. I always like to start with an incident from the character's youth and build from there. For example:

> When Joan was six her best friend had an accident. Well, it wasn't really an accident. The truth is that Joan saw her friend riding a new bicycle and grew intensely jealous. Joan's family couldn't afford a bicycle and Joan had always wanted one. When she saw

Gail riding that bike, Joan was taken up by a sudden hurt that exploded into an uncontrollable rage. Without thinking, she picked up the nearest thing she could find—a large rock—and threw it directly at Gail. It hit her on the leg, her bike went out of control, and Gail plowed head first into a hedge, fell over, and broke her leg.

Joan ran away before Gail could see who threw the rock but that didn't mean Joan didn't feel guilty about the whole thing. Joan grew more distant from Gail and their relationship was changed forever. That guilt followed Joan through all her school years and unfortunately, so did her terrible rages. She'd explode, do horrid things, and then regret them later. This made her misanthropic and fearful, but she couldn't help herself. As her rages escalated, so did her guilt until she was entirely incapacitated. And then she met Mark.

My bio story goes on to describe her relationship with Mark, who also flew into rages, but the difference was that he didn't feel the guilt. Soon they were an item and before too long went on a kind of rage-spree that created all kinds of chaos.

The short script will take place in a halfway house where Joan has been placed after release from prison. It's about how a relationship with a counselor there helps her turn her life around. From my prose back story I can use the fact that she has a big connection with Mark, who taught her not to feel guilty that she has never had a bicycle, that her family was poor, that she gets jealous easily, and that she was early on capable of making friends. That's quite a lot of information that could help me in my short script without actually appearing in the script.

And because the script will be short, from the onset I've got to demonstrate Joan's personality and proclivities. I don't have much time so I've got to know her psychology pretty well. That's why, in addition to my prose character backstory, I need to use a character template, and because character is usually expressed through emotion that reacts to situations or creates them, I will have to know how my character experiences certain emotions and displays them. Having an effective character template helps with that. For each emotion, a paragraph will key us in to how the character demonstrates a particular trait and the reasons for it.

Character Template

Sorrow/Grief

Jane masks her sorrow with anger. When she's sad, she feels vulnerable and she hates to feel vulnerable. That's why she gets mad instead of sad. And the sadder the situation, the madder she gets.

Joy

Jane has trouble feeling joy, but when she does she delights in it and wants to share it. Unfortunately she finds this difficult because of her lack of friends, so she expresses it in the only way she knows how . . . by singing. Singing has been her consolation and her solace, and she uses it whenever she feels afraid or lonely. She also uses it when she's happy, though that's not very often.

The rest of the template appears next.

Once you've got a solid backstory prose piece and a completed biography template, you can use the information from that to build solid and complete characters that will give your story greater meaning and impact.

Exercise

Complete the following template for your two main characters.

Sorrow/Grief

Joy

Anger/Rage
Fear
Love
Frustration
Hope
Greed
Loss

Now based on these emotions, write about your two main characters' feelings about, reaction to, and experiences with the following:

Authority
Women/Men (Sex)
Poverty
Wealth
Injustice
Violence
Honesty/Truth
Pleasure
Pain

Next, choose the specific characteristics you want to emphasize in your short script. Remember, you need to really understand your characters but you may not be able to demonstrate all their characteristics in a short script. Your understanding and knowledge of them will provide important subtext even though in your particular short script you may only be able to overtly demonstrate some of their proclivities.

And because you're not writing a feature, you need to keep in mind that you might not have the time to develop these characters as slowly as you'd like to. So remember to use the "tricks" demonstrated by *The Big Lebowski* and *Pirates of the Caribbean* to do that visually and quickly.

You don't need to be elaborate—just inventive and visual.

7. Minimize Characters

Short films can't have huge casts. Because we're pinpointing stories and don't have much time to develop characters, we can only concentrate on three at the most. Writers who fill their short scripts with too many characters end up confusing audiences and trivializing their stories with what they think is necessary character interplay instead of moving the plot forward and creating substance.

Keep on the lookout for characters you can get rid of because they don't really contribute to the story. Characters like waiters, siblings, parents, or gaggles of pals may not really make much difference to the scene. Writers often forget characters they've introduced by leaving them out of scenes even if they are in the room when the main characters interact. That's a good reason to axe them. We'll see how to do that in Chapter 6.

Exercise

Check your script for characters that are just standing around while the principals are speaking or involved in the action. Get rid of them and see what happens. You'll often find that your scene is leaner, meaner, and much more effective.

8. Minimize Locations

Shorts don't have the time to bounce from place to place. Too many locations in a short can confuse audiences and make for a jumpy film. You've got to get to the meat of a scene quickly and elegantly, and that's difficult to do if you have lots of scenes in lots of different places. Those places will also add considerable expense to your budget and increase your shooting time drastically. If you have lots of locations, you'll also require so much editing that your film might look scattered and it may throw your pace off. Better to have your scenes filled with action instead of making that action consist of changing locations. Think carefully about what various locations will add to your story. If they are essential, then use them. If they are only so much window dressing, eliminate them.

Where you set your story is, of course, important. But that depends on what your story is really about. If, for example, the location is a character in your story (if your story is about truckers, you'll have to go on the road in trucks or if it's about fishermen, you'll have to use boats), you are kind of stuck. The key here is to cheat locations whenever you can by intimating them without actually having to work in them.

For example, if you do have a trucker movie, maybe you can get away with creating a truck cab in the sound stage and doing your interiors there. You can use stock footage of trucks on highways (pricey but not so much as actually renting a big-rig), and you can cheat by shooting close. But keep in mind that unless the location is important to your character and story, you can always change it.

If your story is about a trucker in conflict with his wife because he's away so much, you might not even need to show him in the truck necessarily. You might want to concentrate more on the relationship and the arguments involved instead of showing how the guy actually spends his time. This requires you to again keep uppermost in your mind what your story is really about.

Sometimes locations actually get in the way of stories by providing too many opportunities to waste time by exploring that location. Although you might be attracted to long lazy shots of a truck barreling down a deserted highway at night, you need to decide what that shot will actually do for your story. How badly do you need it? Will it further the plot or the character? Is it essential to your message? If you've decided that you can't do without it, prepare to spend the money. Sometimes it can't be helped, but more often it can.

I had a graduate student who was making a film about illegal aliens being smuggled across the Mexican border in a truck. Initially, he was going to rent a truck and shoot in that because most of the shots were interiors. This would have cost plenty. After discussion, he decided to build a truck interior on the sound stage and use a truck only for a couple of shots when exteriors were called for. This saved him hundreds of dollars and didn't interfere with the story.

Keep in mind that certain locations can create huge problems. It's best not to use them if you can help it. Horror can happen anywhere you shoot. That's what insurance is for. But some things are just irreplaceable. So think about the places where those things might be. Irreplaceable objects can all go up in smoke, so to speak, and your careers along with them. Try and cheat those locations wherever you can by shooting tight or simply re-creating or changing the venue. More on this in Chapter 6.

9. Keep Dialogue Pithy

Dialogue isn't easy to write. That's because language is varied and complicated. Every person talks in a different way. That means each character in your script needs to talk in a different way and that creates a definite problem for the writer. How can we differentiate characters by the way they speak if we have little time to develop their characters in a short script? This is pretty challenging, and there is no simple way to do that. Here's a little game I play with students and it works well.

Exercise

Dialogue "Game"

Come up with two unrelated professions.
(Example: Lawyer and Garbage collector)

Have them engage in an encounter with each other (adversarial or not) solely through dialogue.

Example:

>   LAWYER
>
>   I'm chagrined! Each week I dis-
>   tinctly put out three cans and each
>   week you only empty two. Why are
>   you doing this to me?
>
>
>   GARBAGE COLLECTOR
>
>   Wadaya king of da street or somthin?
>   City says you're only allowed two
>   cans. I'm not breakin' my back for
>   fat cats like youse!

This example is a little obvious but we can clearly delineate classes, for example, simply by their vocabulary. I realize that I'm generalizing that garbage collectors are poorly educated, but for the sake of this exercise, please forgive the generalization. I'm merely pointing out that you can use vocabulary to establish a subtext background that includes character. In this example, for instance, we can surmise the garbage collector's view of the people on his route, and that he is very aware of the economic inequality between him and his "clients," and that he resents this.

Conversely, we can see that the lawyer is a person who tends to take things personally and who also believes that the "rules" don't apply to him (re: the two-can limit). This can make for an interesting story down the road that can be quite funny or poignant. And keep in mind that we've created a specific language roadmap for actors to follow when they deliver the lines. They may not say the lines exactly as written, but they will know how to deliver them to keep to the specific character's style of speaking.

In this way we've used dialogue to convey character and further our story and we've done it quickly. We could have been even shorter and just had the lawyer ask why the collector was only emptying two cans, but if we did that we'd lose some of the character development—he takes things personally and uses "fancy" language. You've got to be careful and not make your dialogue so short that it becomes throw-away or staccato.

Avoid Throw-Away Dialogue

Some writers have a knee-jerk propensity to write throw-away dialogue. This is dialogue that is entirely unnecessary to further character or story and is usually entirely reactive or space filling.

For example:

```
                    JOE
     I met a really cool chick at the
     club last night.

                    BILL

     Oh?

                    JOE
     She was really slutty and we ended
     up hooking up. I'll never see her
     again but man what a night! Want
     her number?

                    BILL

     Sure.

                    JOE

     555-1730
```

Bill hauls off and punches Joe in the face.

```
                    JOE (Cont'd)
       What was that for?

                    BILL
       She's my sister.
```

Lots of throw-aways here. We can make this scene a lot shorter and more dynamic like this:

```
                    JOE
       I met a cool chick at the club last
       night. She was really slutty and
       we hooked up. I'll never see her
       again. Do you want her number?
```

Joe pulls a crumpled slip of paper out of his pocket and hands it to Bill. Bill looks at it and punches Joe in the face.

```
                    BILL
       You pervert! She's my sister!
```

"Oh," "sure," the verbal phone number, and "what was that for" are all throw-aways that can be compressed into a much smoother verbal exchange. Make sure that every piece of dialogue counts for something. This is true in features but especially true in a short script. Every word coming out of the character's mouth should reveal character or further the plot in some way. Furthering the plot, however, doesn't mean that it can be ultra-expository.

Limit and Finesse Exposition

Sometimes we do need exposition. We may be writing a sci-fi about a future world and need some exposition to explain that world or its workings. We may need to be expository about how a piece of complicated equipment works or even tell a character's backstory because that backstory is crucial to the current situation.

For the most part, however, exposition needs to be hidden or presented in such a way that we get a greater insight into the character delivering it and at the same time further our understanding and enjoyment of the story.

A common mistake is, of course, when characters tell the audience what's happened in the past when both characters know it. For example:

> HUSBAND
>
> Remember our wedding where that bridesmaid fainted and I had to give her mouth to mouth? I ran into her today.
>
> WIFE
>
> Yeah. I've been talking to her too, and she said she's never forgotten that and neither have I. You were way too eager to do that. I was suspicious then. Now I'm even more suspicious because I found out you've been cheating on me.

UGH! Of course the wife remembers the incident. This is all for the audience's benefit and takes us out of the story. This dialogue is too obvious and not engaging. We can say the same thing much more effectively:

> HUSBAND
>
> I ran into Gloria today.
>
> WIFE
>
> Ah—my fainting bridesmaid.
>
> HUSBAND
>
> Why do you keep harping on that wedding thing?

> WIFE
> Because Clara saw both of you in
> Luigi's and she says Gloria must
> have passed out again because you
> were giving her mouth to mouth!

Now this becomes a plot point too in that the wife has discovered the husband has been cheating. It also reveals character on the part of the wife because of her snide comment. If characters ask each other to remember (unless it's an obscure thing), you can be sure that you are writing that for the benefit of the audience and not those characters.

Make Thoughts Visual

The *only* way we know what's going on in a screenplay is by what characters say or do. A screenplay is not a novel so we can't go on and on telling the audience what the character is thinking. Shakespeare popularized the soliloquy to let audiences know that and it worked then but not so much now. Some writers do make the stylistic decision to let audiences know what characters are thinking through voiceover. That's okay if it appears throughout the movie. Think of Terence Malik's *Days of Heaven*. Voiceover was a mainstay of that film, and it worked really well, even making the movie a stylistic icon. But usually, voiceover is a crutch and should be used with great discretion. At its worst it's used to "describe" what's going on in the visuals. Visuals should be strong enough to stand alone.

You can show us what characters are thinking by how they behave. It's always more effective to demonstrate a character's anger by having him kick a chair or say, "I'm so angry I could eat an iguana!" than by having him say in voiceover, "I was so angry I threw a temper tantrum" and then showing the tantrum. It's also possible to demonstrate a character's decision-making process effectively through some clever visuals.

For example, in the Academy Award–winning screenplay *Juno*, Juno makes the decision not to get an abortion in a rather clever and highly visual sequence of events. First, when she arrives at the clinic she sees a lone protester (Su-Chin) holding up a sign reading "No Babies Like Murdering." Through some conversation we discover that the protester is a classmate and we also discover that Juno has had her share of "mental" issues she doesn't want to talk about. As she continues toward the clinic Su Chin keeps haranguing her.

```
                    SU CHIN
    Your baby has a beating heart, you
    know. It can feel pain. It has
    fingernails!
    Juno turns on the word fingernails.
                    JUNO
    Really? Fingernails?
    She pauses to think and keeps going
    into the clinic.
```

In the next scene she's greeted by a blasé receptionist who feigns concern as she texts. That doesn't deter Juno, and she sits down to fill out forms. Now sound enriches the scene because as Juno looks around at all the pregnant women in the room, she notices little else but their fingernails scratching and picking as the audience hears enhanced sounds of that scratching and picking. Suddenly she gets up and bolts. She hasn't said a word but entirely through visuals and their accompanying sound, we know that she has changed her mind. As she runs out of the clinic Su Chin shouts after her "God appreciates your miracle!" Juno doesn't answer.

This is a really skillful demonstration of how visuals can be used to indicate a character's state of mind. The next scene does have her explaining her decision to her friend but that's an afterthought. The powerful realization has come across, and the audience gets it without the main character having to say a word!

The atmosphere of the clinic helped in that. So you can do a lot with atmosphere in a short film to give the audience information and move your story forward. And so does the action of the characters before, while, and after they speak.

Enhance Dialogue with Visuals

Screenwriters need to think like filmmakers. I find that my screenwriting students refuse to read action that occurs between bits of dialogue because they really want to hear what characters have to say. To production students, those action lines are important because they fill out the look of the film and provide a great deal of subtext. Screenwriters who want to write for production need to learn this to get a better grip on their movie and to better visualize the film. Writers who don't do that are not visualizing enough.

Don't overdo the action between dialogue bits, but keep it in mind because it is vital for giving a visual sense during dialogue exchanges and informing those exchanges. It cuts down the danger of boring and static shots focused on speakers who aren't doing much, and it includes valuable reaction shots, which sometimes are desperately needed. For example:

```
                    RACHAEL
          I'm leaving you and moving in with
          Dave.


                    ARTHUR
          But Dave is a loser and he smokes!
```

Okay, we would like/need to see Arthur's reaction to Rachael's bombshell. Better to write:

```
                    RACHAEL
          I'm leaving you and moving in with
          Dave.

          Arthur's face contorts. He slumps
          into the nearest chair and puts his
          head in his hands.
```

> ARTHUR
>
> But Dave is a loser and he smokes!

Now we know by his actions that Arthur is truly devastated by the news.

Action lines can be very useful in breaking up large chunks of dialogue. Because audiences don't necessarily want to see monologues, we need to give some visual oomph to them by breaking them up. You can go only so long before you need some movement in your shot. It matters little that the character holding forth moves his arms or flails or uses other body language. The important thing here is to realize that huge blocks of dialogue are repugnant to those who read scripts and those who watch films. Instead of launching into soliloquies, use pauses and actions to punctuate and enrich your characters' rants.

As an example, let's look at a speech by the Duchess of Berwick from Oscar Wilde's *Lady Windermere's Fan*. It was written in 1892, but it's still amusing (Wilde, 2005, pp. 15–16). Even though it's from a different medium, I purposely chose it because of its complexity and length. Here's the original written as movie dialogue:

> DUCHESS OF BERWICK
>
> Ah, what indeed, dear? That is the point. He goes to see her continually, and stops for hours at a time, and while he is there she is not at home to anyone. Not that many ladies call on her, dear, but she has a great many disreputable men friends—my own brother particularly, as I told you—and that is what makes it so dreadful about Windermere. We looked upon him as being such a model husband, but I am afraid there is no doubt about it. My dear nieces—you know the Saville girls, don't you?—such nice domestic creatures—plain,

DUCHESS OF BERWICK (CONT'D)

dreadfully plain—but so good—well, they're always at the window doing fancy work, and making ugly things for the poor, which I think so useful of them in these dreadful socialistic days, and this terrible woman has taken a house in Curzon Street, right opposite them—such a respectable street, too! I don't know what we're coming to! And they tell me that Windermere goes there four and five times a week—they see him. They can't help it—and although they never talk scandal, they—well, of course—they remark on it to everyone. And the worst of it all is that I have been told that this woman has got a great deal of money out of somebody for it seems that she came to London six months ago without anything at all to speak of, and now she has this charming house in Mayfair, drives her ponies in the Park every afternoon and all—well, all—since she has known poor dear Windermere. It's quite true, my dear. The whole of London knows about it. That is why I felt it was better to come and talk to you, and advise you to take Windermere away at once to Homburg or to Aix, where he'll have something to amuse him, and where you can watch him all day long. I assure you, my dear, that on several occasions after I was first married, I had to pretend to be very ill, and was obliged to drink the most unpleasant mineral waters, merely to get Berwick out of town. He was so extremely susceptible. Though I am bound to say he never gave away any large sums of money to anybody. He is far too high-principled for that!

As you can see right away, this is a very daunting chunk to get through. The temptation is to skip a lot of it, particularly since it's in a kind of style that isn't in modern speech. But it contains an important bit of exposition—Mr. Windermere is keeping a naughty girl and spending lots of cash on her, and Lady Windermere is just being told about it! As it gives rise to what Lady Windermere will do next, skipping over this would be disastrous to the understanding of the plot.

Breaking this up would have helped considerably! For example:

> DUCHESS OF BERWICK
>
> Ah, what indeed, dear? That is the point. He goes to see her continually, and stops for hours at a time, and while he is there she is not at home to anyone.

The duchess shakes her head sadly and clicks her tongue.

> DUCHESS OF BERWICK (CONT'D)
>
> Not that many ladies call on her, dear, but she has a great many disreputable men friends—my own brother particularly, as I told you—and that is what makes it so dreadful about Windermere. We looked upon him as being such a model husband, but I am afraid there is no doubt about it.

She gazes longingly at Windermere's portrait hanging on the wall behind Lady Windermere and sighs deeply. Lady Windermere looks perplexed and opens her mouth to speak but the duchess is relentless.

> DUCHESS OF BERWICK (CONT'D)
>
> My dear nieces—you know the Saville girls, don't you?—such nice domestic creatures—plain, dreadfully plain—but

> DUCHESS OF BERWICK (CONT'D)
>
> so good—well, they're always at the window doing fancy work, and making ugly things for the poor, which I think so useful of them in these dreadful socialistic days, and this terrible woman has taken a house in Curzon Street, right opposite them—such a respectable street, too!
> I don't know what we're coming to!

Lady Windermere shakes her head and is about to speak again when the duchess presses on.

> DUCHESS OF BERWICK (CONT'D)
>
> And they tell me that Windermere goes there four and five times a week—they see him. They can't help it—and although they never talk scandal, they—well, of course—they remark on it to everyone.

The duchess takes a handkerchief out of her ample bosom and mops her brow.

> DUCHESS OF BERWICK (CONT'D)
>
> And the worst of it all is that I have been told that this woman has got a great deal of money out of somebody, for it seems that she came to London six months ago without anything at all to speak of, and now she has this charming house in Mayfair, drives her ponies in the park every afternoon and all—well, all—since she has known poor dear Windermere.

Lady Windermere looks appalled. She fans herself furiously and shakes her head but the duchess doesn't notice and goes in for the kill.

                    DUCHESS OF BERWICK (CONT'D)
          It's quite true, my dear. The whole
          of London knows about it. That is
          why I felt it was better to come
          and talk to you, and advise you to
          take Windermere away at once to
          Homburg or to Aix, where he'll have
          something to amuse him, and where
          you can watch him all day long.

She reaches out and pats Lady Windermere's hand sympathetically.

                    DUCHESS OF BERWICK (CONT'D)
          I assure you, my dear, that on
          several occasions I after I was
          first married, I had to pretend to
          be very ill, and was obliged to
          drink the most unpleasant mineral
          waters, merely to get Berwick out
          of town. He was so extremely sus-
          ceptible. Though I am bound to say
          he never gave away any large sums
          of money to anybody. He is far too
          high-principled for that!

The scene plays much better broken up. And obviously this speech is meant to reflect the character of the duchess as well as the flavor of the times and give the audience some laughs in the process. This demonstrates how to break up dialogue in general. Now it's important to consider how to say what you want to say in a short film without having to go to such lengths. You'd have to shorten a speech like this dramatically while still leaving in the salient points.

Exercise

This isn't easy. Shorten Lady Berwick's speech to its minimum leaving in character indicators, salient points and the laughs. You can modernize it as well!

Make Dialogue Character Inclusive

Some writers get so caught up in an interchange between two people in the room they lose other characters that may be present. For example, they may begin a scene with three or four characters in a room but once an interchange gets going with two of the characters, the other two people somehow disappear. If other characters are in the scene at its opening, either lose them by having them leave or include them in the action breaking away between dialogue. Interspersing the action really takes care of you later on when you are actually shooting and in post. Even if you don't use some of the action you shoot, you'll have enough coverage in case other problems arise. If you write the scene using other characters as cutaways you give yourself a nice little bit of just-in-case.

10. Exploit Atmosphere

Atmosphere can do a lot for your film. It defines genre and mood, but also it can really move your story where you want it to go quickly and easily, especially in a short film. From the first image on the screen, the audience can be catapulted into the feeling of the film if that image is powerful, evocative, and redolent with the things you intend to explore. For instance, the first establishing shot of a rundown creepy mansion has for eons represented a horror scenario. Your movie may not have a creepy mansion in it but you still want to chill us right away and spook us.

Consider the early Tim Burton film *Sleepy Hollow*. Burton's a master of atmosphere, and in this film Andrew Kent Walker and Tom Stoppard's opening scene is shot to spook. Even the opening credits are presented in a potentially scary way with lots of wavy letters emerging from smoke under ponderous music. This takes about half a minute. Then the film begins.

The first shot is of what looks like drops of blood. We soon learn that these drops are sealing wax on a contract—an ancient-looking thing completed in a dark room. We wonder what's going on and then we're plunged into a scene filled with mist in which a carriage rolls along a road flanked by dead vegetation. The coach is driven by a mysterious rider and is going along at a fast clip while inside, a decrepit aristocrat in wig and brocade jacket looks fearfully around. This is accompanied by the same ponderous music.

As he looks out the carriage window, the aristocrat looks terrified. His eyes focus on a figure, which turns out to be a scarecrow with the head of a pumpkin. Suddenly, lightning flashes and thunder rumbles. A weird metallic sound captures the aristocrat's attention. He looks outside and up at the coach driver who is now HEADLESS!

The aristocrat blanches and leaps out of the coach. He runs through the overgrown field terrified and stops short at the pumpkin-headed scarecrow. He shudders as a metallic sound rings out again. The pumpkin is splattered with blood! This opening sequence takes 2 minutes and 45 seconds and firmly establishes the kind of film we're going to see.

This is interesting because the script actually starts with the next scene in the film—a wharf in the dark. This carriage ride opening was to set the tone and atmosphere firmly in the audience's mind from the onset and to create curiosity and it does just that.

Tim Burton uses atmosphere to good advantage in all of his films. Consider this when you write and shoot your movie. Because you're writing a short film, you don't have time for a premovie atmosphere grab. That means you'll have to incorporate your atmosphere establishment in the first moments of your movie.

We can, in fact, think of the opening sequence of the Burton movie as the first act in a short. We establish atmosphere and the mystery (we can shorten the carriage ride) and then the second act can go on to establish a character intent on solving the mystery and finding a chief clue. The third act can be a solution to that mystery. In any case, the crucial atmosphere of the film has been established and audiences have bought into the dynamics right from the start.

11. Shun Subplots

In a feature, subplots make great transitions and can allow for the main plot to simmer. Shorts have no time for simmering. There is absolutely no room for a subplot in a short. Subplots involve other characters and additional plot points so they are too cumbersome and time consuming to fit into a short film. We'll see that in a later chapter when we demonstrate how to create a short film based on a feature. A short film deals in the essence of a story. It can only deal with one storyline at a time!

12. Save Money

This seems like a pretty obvious commandment, but you'd be surprised how many people I know who've spent thousands and thousands of dollars on their short films in the hopes that they could somehow convince people by sheer force of cash on the screen alone that a feature was in their future. Frankly, people who fund features are looking to save money so they won't be incredibly impressed by an elaborate show of wealth in a short. If you want to impress and have your short act as a feature springboard then the more important thing is the story—how it's executed—than how it looks. If you're making your short to show off your technical skills, you'll need to make sure it's technically wonderful, but story and its execution are still the most important things. We'll speak more of making your film specifically to showcase your strengths later on. Right now, though, keep in mind that you don't want to break the bank and exhaust your future resources . . . resources you may want to use to fund that feature.

I had a few students who learned this the hard way. One person spent $45,000 on her 10-minute short—she hired professionals and used elaborate costumes in a period piece. The film looked great but went nowhere because the story and direction were weak. Keep in mind that Hollywood has incredible technical resources. Lots of people are available to make a film look good, and there's lots of money available to hire the best cinematographers, production designers, and costumers, but studios and production companies are always on the lookout for that scarce thing, *originality*, and stories that really compel and work. That's what you'll need to get a foot in the door. The rest is eye candy and can be bought. So demonstrate your talent in the right areas and NOT in how much money you can throw on the screen. And speaking of money. . .

Reference

Wilde, Oscar. *Lady Winderemere's Fan*. London: Nick Hern Books, 2005.

5
MONEY CHANGES EVERYTHING

I'm assuming you're not made of money, but I've met lots of people who've spared no expense to get their short made. There was the assistant director who was so desperate to get to direct something that he called in favors and mortgaged his house to spend over $30,000 on a short. It looked great, but the only problem was that the script (which he got someone else to write) wasn't great so it went nowhere. There was a graduate student who had a generous rich boyfriend who gave him $75,000 to spend on his 30-minute short that looked fabulous but fell flat because the story didn't work. In spite of advice from lots of people to ditch that particular script, he was married to it so he went ahead. The film went nowhere and, sadly, neither did he. This was a big gamble that didn't pay off.

I'm going to repeat what I said in the last chapter because it's that important! The industry has lots of competent people who can make a film look fabulous, but there's a real demand for unique stories skillfully told. If the story works, Hollywood can hire people to make it look great. That's why screen writers have an advantage. The better the story, the more chance people will spark to it and to you.

I'm not discounting production value. Your film can't be a shoddy piece of work. It can't be sloppy or badly produced. It can't be out of focus. All the things that make movies watchable have to work. If they don't, the story will suffer. Audiences will be distracted and pulled out of the story by serious (and sometimes not-so-serious) production issues. But that doesn't mean you've got to spend lots of money for your film to be competent and watchable. You've just got to be smart about it. That's where compromise comes in.

I'm not talking about thematic compromises here. I'm talking about compromises that will fit your story into a produceable framework without breaking the bank or extending your running time.

Let's look at specific budget breakers and see how you can address them without messing with your story too much.

Budget Breakers

Locations

LIBRARIES

It's almost impossible to get permission to shoot in a library. That's because wary librarians who are understandably protective of their books know that horrible things can and do happen during shoots no matter how careful people are. For example, a student crew was given permission to shoot in our school library. During that shoot, the lights ran hot and WHAM! Suddenly the sprinkler system was activated and the water damage in the shoot area was considerable. From that moment on, no one was ever given permission to shoot in the library again. And this isn't an isolated case. If the scene absolutely has to be in the library, you should rent some shelves and books and make the production designer earn her keep by making it all look real.

MUSEUMS AND ART GALLERIES

A student of mine really needed to shoot in an art gallery because his story was about an artist who had an important show there. He rented a large empty room and filled the walls with paintings by his creative friends and family. The paintings weren't really gallery quality but long shots and soft focus stopped the audience from judging or noticing.

Of course, all the art had to be framed and that was expensive but if you *absolutely* need that environment for your scene, you will have to spend the money. That's why you have to be dead sure that your locations are all very essential to your characters and your story.

CHURCHES, TEMPLES, MOSQUES, ETC.

Scenes in places of worship are notoriously expensive to shoot. Avoid using them if you can. Some of those places can be film friendly, but again, precious objects are often stored there and if they get broken, woe unto you! Also, because places of worship are considered sacred spaces, their ministers, priests, rabbis, or imams may not want their sites desecrated by allowing filming there. And scenes shot (particularly weddings and funerals) there are notoriously expensive for other reasons. I've broken these down next.

BARS

Bars can be tough because of the hours they keep. I had one student convince a bar owner to let him rent the place off hours. It cost about $500 (a good deal), but all filming had to be done between 2 a.m. and 6 a.m. when the bar opened again. And believe it or not, people were lined up outside the bar at 5:45 a.m. waiting to get in! Not much time to get every shot.

And naturally bars usually don't allow you to use their products, so filmmakers have to provide the props, which can be problematic depending on the number of people they want in the scene. Also, lighting takes a while and eats up much of the shooting time. It's probably easier to re-create a bar on a sound stage where you have time to fiddle, light, and explore shot options. Mistakes happen when you're in a hurry.

OFFICES AND OFFICE CUBICLES

Offices are notoriously problematic. Most office buildings have security issues that won't allow crews to take them over. And in addition, dressing sets in existing offices can be virtually impossible because people don't like their stuff moved. If you're willing to leave everything alone and use the office as is, you might be lucky, but you'll often have to hire the building security guard to watch your every move and a cleaning crew to mop up after you. And you'll be forced to shoot at night or on weekends and often have to pony up a hefty fee to do that.

GROCERY STORES, DRUG STORES, CAR REPAIR SHOPS, RETAIL SHOPS

These locations create major issues. Supermarkets are usually always open and don't want you messing with their business. If you want to shut one down for a shoot, you'll be paying that hefty fee. And you'll also have to pay a fee to a mom-and-pop bodega as well. You'll have to shell out at any of these locations, and again, you'll have to shoot when the businesses are closed and you'll have to provide security and insurance assurance. If you really need locations like these (they are difficult to fake because of all the necessary merchandise, equipment, etc.), you might have to bite the financial bullet and shell out.

Think about what you want to say in the scene and if you really need the store interior. This is crucial. Go for meaning over atmosphere if you can help it! If you do that, you'll always find another way to say what you need to say in a much easier and cost-efficient way. For example, I had a student who wanted to demonstrate a character's obsessive-compulsive disorder (OCD) complex by having him inside a grocery store fiddling and arranging purchases in the checkout line, driving the customer behind him crazy. To solve the problem of grocery store access, I suggested that it would be so much easier to have his OCD guy in the store parking lot instead with a cart of groceries, maddeningly rearranging them in his car while another car idled nearby, desperate for his parking space.

My student saved money and a hassle and got his point across. All he needed was his own car, his friend's car, and a few cereal boxes and soda cans sticking out of brown paper bags! Money was saved, lighting problems eliminated, and shooting time drastically reduced.

PUBLIC BUILDINGS

Public buildings present several problems. First, you've got to secure proper permits, and some cities don't allow shooting in public buildings. This means you'll have to cheat an exterior by "labeling" a building, and you'll have to get permission to do that if you want to actually do it. You can, of course, cheat it in other ways. But that's for exteriors. If you want interiors, you've got another whole set of issues to confront.

If you need to use a courthouse, for example, you'll be faced with outrageous challenges of use permission. Lots of scripts I've seen have had attorney discussions taking place in the lobby of the courthouse. These discussions could take place in a hall outside a courtroom—much easier to cheat in a nondescript hallway that can be easily conjured up without the headaches of a public lobby location. Unfortunately, many filmmakers think that the look of the environment where such discussions take place is extremely important. Really? Again, it's important to remember why the discussion is taking place and the significance of that discussion. The background may not matter at all, so if you don't have the luxury of spending lots of time and money getting that lobby shot just for appearances, lose it!

Courtrooms themselves are a little more problematic and harder to cheat, but they can be re-created on a sound stage. This might be a real pain, but if your script centers around a trial, you'll need to do it. The courtroom can be simple. It's not always necessary to create a grand and elaborate structure!

PRISONS

Forget about getting permission to shoot in an actual prison. Instead, cheat this location in several ways. A visiting room is pretty easy. You can use any large room that's got chairs, tables, and some vending machines. You can even lose the vending machines if you don't need them.

Cells are also cheatable, although you'll have to get a pretty savvy production designer to work with you. I had one student who created the bars on a cell by using paper towel tubes glued together and spray painted. It worked surprisingly well! And besides, people were more interested in what was going on in the cell, so the bars simply faded as the camera moved in on the prisoner.

You may want to shoot cell block interaction complete with workout rooms, dining halls, and common areas with cell backgrounds. This is not advisable and will create a real nightmare for you. Consider writing your sequences in manageable areas and without extreme wide shots. If you go in tight, you'll get the claustrophobic prison feel you need without springing for the impossible backgrounds that you can't afford.

You might be able to find cafeterias to shoot in, but they'll have to be simple and stripped down. And then you'll have a nightmare setting up food, etc. Best to focus on your interaction while eating instead of while getting food. For example, in my prison movie I might have written the following scene to show animosity between Mark and Ernie.

INT. PRISON CAFETERIA – DAY

> MARK and ERNIE, sandwiched in a line of hungry prisoners, sluggishly move along a serving station. Their trays are nearly full. At the last station, a BURLY WORKER slops some dessert goop on Ernie's tray.
>
> Ernie sticks his finger in the goop and frowns. The worker ignores him. Ernie fills his spoon with the goop, turns, and flings it at Mark. Mark picks up his fork and jams it into Ernie's hand.

To shoot this, I will have to include a line of prisoners, a cafeteria serving station, and a burly worker. Quite a setup! If I write the scene in a different way, I'll save myself having to get all those things and I can still make my point. Written for production, the scene could go like this:

INT. PRISON CAFETERIA – DAY

>MARK, 58 and prison worn, carrying a tray of suspicious-looking food, finds a seat at a table near ERNIE, 35 and anxious. He sits down and picks up his fork. Just as he's about to dig in, a bread roll hits him in the eye.
>
>He looks up. Ernie is smirking and getting ready to throw another roll. Mark lunges forward and jams the fork into Ernie's hand.

Now I can use sound to indicate a noisy cafeteria and will only need my two principal actors, a couple of tables, some suspicious-looking food on a tray, two bread rolls, and a fork! Much easier to negotiate and no extra casting and prop hassles.

HOSPITALS

There are lots of stories where you might want to have your characters appear in hospitals. You can grab exteriors of hospitals, but you can't shoot in them so you'll have to create a hospital set on a sound stage, and that will cost you lots of money because you'll have to rent expensive equipment and props to make the scene look authentic. If you can write the scene without your character having to lie in a hospital bed, you should try and do that.

If you want to show a character dying, for example, perhaps that character can die at home and your deathbed scene can be just as powerful because of the context. If your character has been injured (leg in bandages, etc.), you could still have that character at home interacting with visitors.

You need to decide how important it is for your character to be seen in a hospital bed. If it's important to your story, then you'll have to spring for the bed, but maybe you won't have to spring for the fake life-support equipment and monitors. Make sure you really need them to make the scene work before you write them in.

SPORTS VENUES

Every so often I get people who want big games to appear in their films. Soccer, Baseball, Football and other sports that require stadiums or arenas are really problematic. You might be able to use facilities at your school if you're a student, but then you've got to get a load of extras to act as spectators (see "crowds" later). And you'll have to get players to play the games so that the whole thing looks real. Better to avoid this by making your story center on the drama around the game and make it so effective that you don't have to show the game itself.

SCHOOLS

Schools will sometimes let you shoot on weekends. You'll have to hire a security guard to be present, but it can be done in some places. However, because of past abuses, some schools in some states have shut down film shoots altogether. The Los Angeles times reported on October 8, that "Los Angeles Unified School District Superintendent Ramon Cortines suspended all commercial film shoots at Los Angeles Unified schools in wake of broadcast reports by KNBC-TV Channel 4 into allegations that film shoots had disrupted classrooms and damages school property. One campus shoot in 2011 was for a pornographic film, the station reported."

Remember, shooting when schools are filled with kids is very problematic. The moment you involve minors in a project you'll have to jump through a lot of hoops and these include getting release forms from parents–something you might not have the time or energy to do.

Events

WEDDINGS

You can create a wedding dynamic by shooting tight and focusing on the aspects of the wedding you chose to emphasize. For example, if you're focused on messed-up vows, you might not need to see hundreds in a church exclaiming. Perhaps only the parents seeing this might suffice. Or shoot tight, making use of only a few crucial wedding guests.

There are lots of costs involved in weddings—even fake ones. Bride and groom get-ups, bridesmaid outfits and groomsmen regalia, church decorations, flowers, and extras to fill in the pews. Better to shoot weddings in gardens or other low-maintenance outdoor locations where you can have people standing around (no chairs to rent) in a simple setting. This assumes that your theme isn't a big fat wedding. If it is, you may be stuck with all the expenses but remember to consider what you are saying in your script. Is it about dynamics and relationships and process, or is it about opulence and extravagance? If it is about the latter you will have to cough up!

FUNERALS

If you must have an indoor funeral, set it in a small room where you can go in close and pretend it's packed with mourners. And remember, caskets, even fake ones, don't come cheap. Try your best not to have a casket in your script. If you can, try to go beyond the funeral right to burial.

You can create a fake grave site in a neutral exterior and you can fake the grave by covering sandbags with a green fuzzy tarp or simply shoot someplace you can dig a hole if you need a hole (it doesn't have to be particularly deep) and have people shovel dirt into it (if you absolutely need that). One of my students had written a script where a burial scene began his story. The mourners were seated in chairs around the grave site as the coffin was lowered into the ground but this created huge budget problems—renting the coffin, getting a grave, etc.

When I urged him to consider what that particular scene was really about and what he wanted to highlight by having it, he realized that it was about grief and the relationship between the family mourners. That helped him to rewrite the scene in a much more economical and efficient way. He had his mourners standing (now he didn't need to rent chairs and set them up) and he began the scene after the coffin was lowered. That way he could fake a grave (using that fuzzy tarp or some dirt) and concentrate on the mourners.

Crowds

People like to write crowds into their scripts to add punch. There are "crowds" at weddings, funerals, parties, parks. There are crowds on city streets and there are crowds struggling to get a look at crime scenes or red carpet affairs. But crowds require lots of extras, and getting lots of extras can be expensive (if you're paying them) and impossible to find if you're not. Nobody has that many friends willing to show up to perform the thankless task of standing around waiting to be a snippet in a short film!

Instead, think about why you want to use crowds. If they are just background and not essential to the scene, you can either lose them or get away with shooting tight. You can have just a few people moving in close in the background. Sometimes this can seem claustrophobic enough to get your point across.

Period Pieces

Lots of us love historical pieces filled with antique locations, fabulous costumes, ornate scenery, and bewitching antiquated lighting. Not good. Period pieces require lots of money from the onset. All those things we love cost a fortune.

Getting the period look right can be very problematic. Props, costumes, and even language of the dialogue can require more work than you're willing or able to do. Ask yourself why this project needs to be set in the past (or future).

I have one student who is particularly fond of period pieces. She wants to do everything in the past. But when I compel her to ask herself what her film is really about, she always discovers that it is about human issues and foibles that can crop up in any century. That's usually the case. The only real reason to do a period piece is if you are re-creating an historical event or basing your story on an historical event. Then you really do have to spring for the trappings of the time period but some time periods and locations that typify them are easier than others.

A World War II drama, for instance, can be shot in old buildings and use fairly simple costumes. It's not a good idea to write in tanks, battalions, old planes, and cars, but if you're telling a human story, it certainly can take place in the 1940s. And you can use guns, old military uniforms, and time-specific costumes.

If you have a fabulous production designer you might be able to build certain environments on set. I had one student doing a submarine drama (similar to the 1981 German submarine classic *Das Boot*), and he was able to cheaply re-create a submarine interior on the sound stage that looked quite realistic, especially when shot close and in low light.

A Western can be shot mostly in exteriors: deserts, brush, wilderness. But there's an important caveat. My students who write Westerns they think they can get away with just costume charges and are willing to scrape together the money for them. Unfortunately, they don't realize that they may vastly increase their budget requirements by adding costs associated with traveling to the wilderness location. And it's not always easy to find old Western cabins, towns, or saloons. There are old Western towns for rent, but these along with crew travel, per diem, and housing really push budgets into the stratosphere. And let's not forget horses!

Animals

Ah the horse! That mainstay of Western movies really gives a piece flavor and authenticity but can also plunge filmmakers into worlds of dusty pain! Using horses on shoots requires animal wranglers, transportation fees, and often, higher insurance costs. If you want to eliminate horses, you can cheat them using sound.

For example, here's a scene using horses:

EXT. HOMESTEAD – DAY

A ramshackle cabin sits in the middle of nowhere. JAKE, 31 and built for work, is chopping wood near the cabin's tilting porch. He's startled at the sound of GALLOPING HORSES. He puts down his axe and watches as a rangy cowboy and a man dressed in black ride up and stop short near him. Their horses are lathered in a long-ride sweat.

The men dismount. Jake looks at them curiously. Suddenly the cowboy rushes forward and grabs Jake. After a struggle, he pins Jake to the ground.

The man in black ambles over and draws his pearl-handled revolver. With slow elegance he butts it up against Jake's temple just as ANABELLE, a worn-out 30, runs out of the cabin.

She SCREAMS at the same time a shot SCREECHES into Jake's brain.

Horses are nice in this scene. They add color and clomping sounds. They indicate the men have ridden far and they provide atmosphere. But let's save some money! Here's how the scene could be rewritten without ponies:

EXT. HOMESTEAD – DAY

A ramshackle cabin sits in the middle of nowhere. JAKE, 31 and built for work, is chopping wood near

> the cabin's tilting porch. He's startled at the SUDDEN SOUND OF HORSES.
>
> He puts down his axe and turns to look when suddenly, he's grabbed by a RANGY COWBOY. They struggle and Jake is pinned to the ground. A MAN in a black coat and overly dusty Stetson ambles over and draws a pearl-handled revolver.
>
> With slow elegance he butts it up against Jake's temple just as ANABELLE, a worn-out 30, runs out of the cabin. She SCREAMS at the same time a shot SCREECHES into Jake's brain.

One might argue that this scene is even more exciting because the attack comes suddenly and out of nowhere. Agile editing can add to this excitement. And the need for horses and their accouterments has disappeared.

Unfortunately, in some cases, horses are necessary. If the next sequence in the previous scenario needs to show the men riding off and if the movie continues to focus on them, horses will have to be included. But if the story focuses on Anabelle and her reaction to her husband's murder, we don't have to show the horses if we write the shooting scene like this:

> With slow elegance he butts it up against Jake's temple and pulls the trigger.
>
> The men run off just as the cabin door flies open. ANABELLE, a worn-out 30, runs out of the cabin, SCREAMS, and rushes over to Jake, cradling him in her arms.

If you can't cut all your horses, cut as many of them as you can. In the sample scene, I might have wanted to have Jake working with horses in a corral or at least seen some tied up near him, but even though the ponies might have made for good atmosphere, they weren't really crucial to the story. If your animals aren't crucial to the story, get rid of them!

And remember, animals don't always want to do what you tell them! I had a student writing a script in which a cat figured prominently as a motivator for the main character to perform a certain action. I urged him to find a different motivator because although there are trained cats and the trainers who train them, they are not financially propitious in most circumstances. Even trained cats are temperamental and don't always follow directions. Human actors are hard enough to deal with! Happily, my student found a different motivator—more internal than furry—and he was saved from what could have been an outrageous cash outlay.

Even animals that just sit there and do nothing will increase your budget. Insurance companies and film schools will still insist on animal wranglers and increased coverage because you never know if Fido will go berserk and bite the leading lady!

Vehicles

CAR WRECKS

If you want to include car accidents in your story, don't show them! Instead write an accident scene this way:

INT. CAR – NIGHT

Margaret drives with one hand while the other hand is busy applying crimson lipstick to her collagen-infused lips. When she's done, she drops the lipstick in her open purse, but it misses the opening and falls to the floor on the passenger's side.

Margaret scowls, ducks her head, and reaches down to retrieve the lipstick. A HORN BLAST. SMASH. A BRIGHT LIGHT.

INT. CAR – CONTINUOUS

Margaret is slumped across the passenger seat, blood oozing from her freshly crimsoned mouth.

If your story demands that the audience see wrecked cars, you can buy some from a wrecking shop, but then you'll have to pay to transport them to your location and set them up and will add money and headaches. Remember, it's the before and after of the accident that is important and not the moment of impact itself!

AMBULANCES

And then there's the issue of ambulances arriving at the crash site. (Or any other site for that matter.) You can cheat ambulances easily by using siren sound. For example, while the shot is on Margaret slumped across the passenger seat, an ambulance siren can scream in the background.

We usually need ambulances present only if a scene inside the ambulance is absolutely necessary to show something that furthers plot or character development as no other scene could. How important is it to see an accident victim being taken away? How important is it to see dead bodies wheeled into a vehicle? If you decide you need an ambulance scene, you could cheat the inside by renting a gurney and emergency medical technician (EMT) equipment and shooting tight inside a small room to re-create the truck's interior.

FIRE TRUCKS

What's true for ambulances is true for fire trucks. We may want to see firemen rush inside a building, but we don't necessarily have to write in their truck. We can cheat scenes using costumes, so when you're writing a fire scene you might want to start it after the firemen have left their truck and are moving toward the building. And again, you can use sirens in the background.

COP CARS

Lots of movies need cops, and if we need them to wear uniforms that will add another wardrobe cost, but that's okay.

They may be essential. We can, however, cheat their cars. Use sound and avoid having us see the actual cars if possible because they will be hugely expensive to rent. I had one graduate student who was able to shoot her film using actual cop cars, but that's because her father was chief of police in a small town and he allowed her to use a couple. He even provided real cops and because they didn't have to act but just rush in or stand around, it all worked. Most of us, though, are not so fortunate. As a rule, it's best to avoid writing cop cars into your script and that includes having them involved in car chases! Not only are car chases dangerous to shoot and would require experienced stunt people, but getting permits and closing down roads to film them is not an option for most filmmakers working on a budget.

SUBWAYS AND BUSES

You can write scenes that take place on running subways and active buses, but you'll probably have to steal them when you shoot them. And if you steal them, you won't be able to shoot them using all your equipment. Better to re-create subway interiors on a sound stage. You can rent a bus, but it will cost you. And then you'll have to cheat the exterior by shooting other buses around town. A hassle, but it can be done. Better to write these scenes as exteriors at bus stops or on subway platforms, although these permits may be difficult to acquire.

BOATS

Unless you're adapting *Moby-Dick* or writing a sea-faring saga (hope not!) boats are not a viable option. The insurance costs will mess you up and so will the weather and rough seas (or any kind of seas for that matter). Swells are not conducive to smooth shooting. If you want to have boats in your movie, make sure the action takes place on the dock and use the boats as background. If you need the look of a claustrophobic boat interior, create it. This will be much cheaper and easier to work with. That way you won't have to block off a marina space or wrangle water.

AIRPLANES

What is true for boats is true for planes. One huge hassle. Create the interior of the plane on a sound stage. And naturally, shooting at airports is a difficulty as well. If you are using a cell phone camera or other small device you can get away with looking like you're shooting a personal video of a departing/arriving friend. Stealing shots is not only a stress Everest, but also iffy.

You can do that if you're adventurous and bold and able to reshoot lots of times on different days, but if you show up at an airport with a crew and try to shoot you'll be squashed like a bug by Transportation Security Administration (TSA) and airport police. Permits aren't handed out easily either. If you desperately need an airport scene for the story to make sense, write it so that it's a quickie and can be grabbed on the run.

TRAINS

You can write a scene on a train's interior because it's easy to re-create on a sound stage, and you can even get an exterior by stealing a shot down at your central station. But know that elongated scenes with crew at train terminals will be a permit and expense disaster and may not be available at all. Better to write your scenes along abandoned tracks. The operative word here is *abandoned*.

We should all be familiar by now with the tragic story of 27-year-old camera assistant Sarah Jones. In February 2014 she was on the set of *Midnight Rider* outside Doctortown, Georgia, as part of a 20-person crew trying to shoot a scene on a live train track. The scene, a dream sequence, called for a bed to be placed on the track. A permit wasn't secured, and the director told the crew that in the highly unlikely event that a train should appear, they'd have 60 seconds to get clear. Sixty seconds wasn't enough. The train showed up unexpectedly. Sarah was killed.

Hollywood director Randall Miller pleaded guilty to involuntary manslaughter. According to the *Los Angeles Times,* on March 2, 2015, Miller, who also pleaded guilty to a charge of criminal trespass, will serve up to two years in the Wayne County Detention Center in Jesup, followed by eight years' probation. He was fined $20,000 and ordered to perform 360 hours of community service.

This incident led to greater awareness about safety on film sets. Should the writer have written the scene on the tracks? Maybe not. Couldn't a dream sequence that featured a trestle be written some other way? If you really want to be certain that your film set will be safe, don't take chances with risky locations. Although it may seem fine to write a scene on an abandoned trestle or in any other precarious place (cliff edges, mountain tops, the edges of tall buildings, etc.), think carefully about the dangers inherent in such locations and make changes accordingly. And ALWAYS get permits!

Stunts

Dangerous locations sometimes involve dangerous stunts. I know of a student who wrote a base-jumping scene into his movie and actually had the nerve to shoot it. He and some friends hiked to a cliff top with gear and handed out GoPros. The scene was startling indeed but the student was incredibly lucky! Think of how he would have felt if a jumper had died during this shoot. Think carefully. Is a movie scene really worth risking a life?

All of these kinds of stunts—hang gliding, bungee jumping, tightrope walking, cliff diving, car or motor bike racing or flipping, leaping from buildings . . . the list is long—can end in tragedy. If you are going to write in a stunt—even a minor one—you'll have to hire a qualified stunt person to execute it. That will cost you money, but it may also complicate your shots because the stunt person will have to double for your actor. Sometimes making the audience believe that your "star" is doing the stunt can be really hard work. You'll have to play with angles, perspective, costumes, and makeup. It may not be worth the bother. Think of ways other than writing in elaborate or dangerous stunts to make your movie exciting and interesting.

And don't forget: Even certain actions taken by your characters that may seem minor (head bumping, falling down, leaping over puddles, etc.) may need stunt people. You need to protect your actors no matter what!

Fights

Fights feature pretty prominently in lots of short films. If you want to write a fight scene, know that you'll have to hire a fight choreographer to make it look right. That means you don't necessarily have to write all the fight moves into the script. Just know that if you write: "Bill and Sam go at each other with fists swinging" it will take some time to shoot that and influence the length of your movie.

Some writers like to include all the moves of a fight, but this is really counterproductive because the fight choreographer will have his or her own ideas. That's why it's a good idea to write that the fight happens and leave the details alone.

If you include a fight and its aftermath, you'll have to include extra makeup costs in your budget. Scars and wounds cost extra. Good makeup is really important. One student movie I watched had the bruising done so badly that the guy looked like he worked in a coal mine and never washed. You don't want this. That's why you'll have to put out extra bucks to get a fabulous makeup person.

If your story can get by without a vicious fight and its result, write the fight out of it. If you need the fight as a story point, you can cut your expenses in half in this area by just showing us the aftermath of the fight so you'll have to spring only for the makeup. But keep in mind that if the fight is necessary and important to show, hiding it in the cut won't work.

Some students want to take the coward's way out when they don't feel comfortable writing a particularly heavy or difficult confrontation and so they write only the preamble and the aftereffects of the confrontation. Not good! By doing that they weaken the story considerably. The audience wants to see the nitty-gritty tough stuff of the film and so you've got to give it to them. Saving money is not an excuse. Bite the bullet and write the scene even if it's expensive. Otherwise, write a different kind of film. Important confrontations, either physical or emotional, should happen on screen so the audience can get the full impact.

That impact sometimes means things get broken. I knew a student who decided he wanted his fighters to break through a plate-glass window. He needed to get safety glass and set it up on the sound stage. Because of the expense and logistics, there could be only one take of that glass break-through. It didn't work right, and he was out lots of money and time. It would have been better to avoid the drama of breaking glass and use instead break-away props (tables, chairs, etc.) that were cheaper and sometimes reusable. If the fight aftermath is necessary, so be it. But often the fight's the thing and the rest is so much window dressing that filmmakers can ill afford.

Weapons

The same is true for weapons. If you use swords and guns, you'll have to budget for these props. If you are writing in guns and your location is on a city street or some other public place, even though the guns are fake, you'll need to have a police officer present. That will add sometimes as much as $800 a day to your budget. That's why it's best to write your fight scenes in private locations you can control where no one will assume your weapons are real. Even then, you may want officer presence. For instance, one of my students was shooting in a private parking garage but it was possible for people to enter that garage and misconstrue the situation. He got an off-duty cop to be present because the peace of mind that gave him was important to reduce the stress level on the set.

Rules for Cheating

1. Decide if the budget breaker is really necessary to the story.
2. Avoid unnecessary wide establishing shots.
3. Start scenes earlier or later to avoid budget-breaking monsters.
4. Use sound as a stand-in for budget breakers.
5. Cheat locations by writing descriptions so that shooting can be tight.

Exercise

Write two scenes from your story: one that includes a major budget breaker and one that cheats to avoid it.

Reference

LA Unified Suspends Commercial Filming at Schools after Reports of Damage, Porn Movie. *Los Angeles Times*, October 8, 2015.

6

KILLING YOUR DARLINGS

We all want our movies to be compelling. We want to engage audiences and make them want to keep watching. One of the enemies of good storytelling is boredom, and heaven forbid we should inflict that on our audiences. So let's consider how we might be doing that in spite of ourselves.

One of the most common mistakes writers make is to include useless transition scenes, which may seem fabulous and necessary when they "see" the movie in their heads but are actually entirely useless, expensive, time killing, and boring!

I took on a project in the Arctic years ago where I taught Inuit and Dene artists to make films about their own culture. That's because network television had moved in north of the 60th parallel and was destroying Inuit and Dene culture. Kids were no longer speaking to their parents in their native language and violence portrayed on television was, for the first time, creeping into heretofore peaceful and tight communities.

My partner and I assembled Inuit and Dene artists from all over the Arctic and began by showing them short films as examples of what they might do. Some of them had never seen a film or a TV show before. When the first film was over we asked the Inuit and Dene what they thought. They gasped in awe. One of them finally spoke. "That man in the story must have been a great wizard," he said reverentially. "What makes you say that?" I asked. The movie had to do with a detective finding a body in a hotel room, jumping into his car and running all over trying to find the killer. "Well, he certainly had magic," said the man, "because one minute he was in a room and the next minute in his car. He must have been able to do this by magic!" They had a similar reaction when we showed them non–Hollywood-type films. When I showed them a short I had written about a girl at a birthday party, they wanted to see the entire party play out. They didn't understand why the piece had to be edited for pacing and story efficiency.

My partner and I were astonished. We never realized we had to define edits because these people didn't know what they were! We had to explain that those mundane parts (traveling, eating, sleeping) were intentionally left out of the movie and happened in the spaces between scenes.

This kind of thinking is foreign to all of us who grew up with movies and TV and that we all understand the nature and purpose of cuts. Really? In spite of all they know, most writers still include scenes that are entirely unnecessary just to get from one location to another.

For example, lots of my beginning students make the following common mistake:

INT. BEDROOM – MORNING

FRANK, 21, looking like a train hit him, is wrapped up in sheets in his bed SNORING loudly when the alarm RINGS. He groans, pounds the clock, and stretches.

INT. BATHROOM – CONTINUOUS

Frank looks in the mirror and growls. He splashes water on his face, brushes his teeth, and pats down his hair.

INT. BEDROOM – CONTINUOUS

Frank stands in front of his open closet door looking at a rack of identical black suits. He squints at each one carefully and then chooses the suit nearest the wall.

INT. HALL - CONTINUOUS

> Frank, fully dressed and looking sharp, walks down the hall.

INT. STAIRWELL - CONTINUOUS

> Frank is halfway down the stairs when the DOORBELL RINGS followed by LOUD KNOCKING. A few seconds later, five police dressed in riot gear, break the door down, YELL, rush up the stairs, drag Frank down to the ground floor, push him onto the carpet, and cuff him.

Whew. Okay. I suppose you could make the argument that we needed to see Frank's routine to get a bit of character. We needed to see all those *identical* suits and we needed to be just as surprised as he was when the cops break in. Maybe in a feature. But in a short you don't have time for all of this. You have time for ONLY what's necessary to the story, and that early stuff isn't really necessary.

Many of my students don't believe they can get their story down into 8 to 10 pages, but after they outline and think a lot about their story, they find they can do that. And especially in the second draft, after they've written 12 pages when they needed 10, they can see what to cut and usually it's the unnecessary transition scenes. They can combine scenes to make a greater impact and create faster pacing, and that's what we want in a short.

Remember that when you shoot, you'll have to do a setup for every slug. That means not only will you have to get a house that has stairs, but you'll also have to light and set up in a bathroom, in a hall, and on a staircase. What a hassle and time killer.

The really important part of this scene is that a guy is surprised by the cops who break in and arrest him. And we can get some of Frank's character in other ways as you'll see in the following fix:

INT. BEDROOM – MORNING

> FRANK, 21, looking like a train hit him, is wrapped up in sheets in his bed SNORING loudly. Next to his bed is a clothes horse fitted out with an immaculate expensive black suit, a crisp white shirt, and an expensive-looking tie. A Rolex watch is on the bedside table next to a bottle of Jack Daniels and a vial of prescription pills.
>
> Frank's own SNORE wakes him slightly and he gulps and turns over.
>
> Suddenly, the bedroom door bursts open and three cops, dressed in riot gear and YELLING WILDLY, drag Frank out of bed, throw him on the floor, and cuff him.

Now we only have one setup (the bedroom) and we have cut our cost by having only one suit instead of a rack. Also, we've found out even more about Frank by having the booze, the Rolex, and the pill vial next to him. And, by the way, Rolex knock-offs are cheap. If you can't afford that, simply lose it and you can fill an empty booze bottle with tea, saving even more money.

We've also cut down the number of cops to save us uniform money and actors! Obviously, this is much more efficient and can be shot quickly. It's a fast, exciting opening for a short film and gets the audience involved right away.

This also saves you looking for a location that includes staircases. Your next scene can be an exterior when the cops throw Frank into a squad car, or to save even more money and time you can simply cut to the cop shop's interrogation room if you want. You don't need those pesky transition scenes. If you do want to give us information before you get to the cop shop, you can do that in a car, but if for some reason you need them to talk in the car (for example, Frank could make a break for it at a red light somehow) and it's an *important* part of the plot, then by all means write the scene. Just know that you'll be paying for that car.

Remember, it's also true that, as some say, the editing process is a second chance at directing, but that's also true for writing. Removing information rather than adding it can sometimes make for a better story, and knowing how to do that will make you a better writer.

Marry Locations

Think carefully about why you need multiple locations to make your point. If you're telling a story that requires a passage of time, you will need various locations to show that. But if your story can be made shorter and more efficient by having lots of the action and dialogue take place in one or two locations, you should do that. If the characters are compelling and the writing tight and interesting, your short will still impress. The idea is to demonstrate how you can tell a story visually and by what characters do and say and not necessarily the number of places they inhabit while doing and saying.

If two characters are in a house having an argument, keep the argument in one room rather than spreading it all over the house. The dialogue should be sparkling enough to indicate movement so that you don't need your actors to change physical locations. Think about the classic film *Who's Afraid of Virginia Woolf?* In that movie director Mike Nichols shot arguing people so dynamically and Ernest Lehman wrote such compelling dialogue that audiences forgot the location and concentrated on the characters' interaction. We didn't need to see the characters running from room to room flinging insults at each other.

Shun Remote Locations

Shooting in a faraway location (even if it's only a few hours' drive away) can be dangerous because if you miss something when you look at your footage, pickups aren't easy to do. Nor is sound. I had one graduate student who wrote her graduate thesis film script with a specific location in Ohio.

She shot it there and when she got back realized that her sound was so bad she had to loop all her dialogue because she didn't have the money to go back and reshoot. Horrible! Not only was this hideously stressful, but it also added an additional expense she hadn't considered.

And sadly, while she was in Ohio she ran into some significant location problems and because her shooting schedule was tight, she quickly decided to cut scenes from the script she later realized were more crucial to her story than she realized. It was too late to do anything about that because she couldn't afford to go back to Ohio to reshoot.

The trick is to consider again how desperately you need the scene to be a particular location and how much that will add to the story and the atmosphere. Sometimes it's necessary to go to a certain specific place, but usually that place can be cheated or perhaps re-created locally. You need to decide if that remote location is in the best interests of your film and your pocketbook. I had a student set on shooting in snow simply for the effect it would create. She was like a dog with a bone on this one and hung onto this notion until I finally showed her how much it would add to her budget (many thousands of dollars!). She gave it up because it wasn't essential to her story, and letting go of snow would help her get her movie made. That's the important thing after all.

Get Rid of Side Characters

Short films can't have lots of characters. Because you don't have much time for character development, you'll need to follow Short Bible Rule #6 and kill your characters or combine them. Ask yourself if you really need a brother and a sister to demonstrate family dynamics. Maybe you can do just as well by having just a brother or a sister or even just mom and dad. I had one graduate student who had a dinner scene with mom, dad, and his main character. He realized he could get along without the mom and just have the dad and son talking. Mom could be in the kitchen off-screen shouting a comment or simply absent in the scene if her existence was never an issue.

Another student had a sheriff stopping a car on the highway and then speaking with the driver. The scene was meant to convey only that the sheriff was crooked and stopped people unnecessarily, taking a bribe to let them go. The student realized he could get rid of the conversation with the driver by showing the sheriff walking up to the car, pausing, taking a roll of bills from an "invisible" passenger, and then walking back to his own vehicle while counting the money. One fewer character and no extra dialogue to lengthen the scene! And he didn't have to show the exterior of the cop car. He could simply show the sheriff inside his car bearing down on the other vehicle with his siren blaring.

Often writers put in extra characters because they think a scene will be made more "realistic" by including them. Frankly, the audience won't notice their absence if you write an action the audience can focus on, an action that will further character or story.

Lose Unnecessary Establishing Shots

Do you really need that establishing shot? Often these shots tout location, location, location when you really want to focus on character, character, character. Establishing shots take up movie and shooting time and don't always add to the story. Unfortunately, they are often boring too. Unless your film is location-centric and unless location functions like a character in your story (e.g., Vegas in a story about gambling), you should consider losing establishing shots.

However, if your establishing shot is a character indicator and helps your subtext, you can use it. For instance, if your establishing shot is an empty bedroom (before a character appears in it) and its decor is very character revealing (posters of Cary Grant, Ninja Turtles, The Mars Rover and assorted naked cover girls on walls painted black and windows covered with aluminum foil), then you probably need that establishing shot to indicate your character is an eclectic strange type. Make sure that you can use this information later in your script (maybe the character's arc dictates that he change the look of his room, ripping down the posters and exchanging them for elaborate banks of fish tanks). Otherwise, we don't really need to see cityscapes, tall office buildings, or acres of saguaros.

Nix the Exotic

Exotic shots take time and money and are just so much eye candy. Do you really need an aerial shot? Do you really need to use a drone to get a fly-by or overhead? Do you really need a helicopter? Do you really need exotic plants or animals? Do you really need a GoPro shot? Do you really need a chase scene involving cars, motorcycles, boats, ocelots? I bet you don't.

Lots of filmmakers get carried away with the groovyness of trick shots and the exotic and waste time and money getting them even though they don't add much to the story. Don't write them in hoping you'll somehow be able to figure out how to use them.

Keep Phone Conversations Short and Visual

For some reason, lots of novice screenwriters love writing one-sided phone conversations without realizing that the shot they create by doing so is a soul-crushing static one. I've read scripts where phone speak goes on for nearly a page with nary a line devoted to movement. I don't care how important you think that phone conversation is, it usually doesn't make for good filmmaking. That's why you should keep these conversations as short as possible and write them in such a way that they hold the audience's interest and contain some movement.

The following is an example.

INT. BEDROOM – DAY

    Doris, wearing a skimpy leopard bikini and Lucite high heels is stretched out on a window seat dialing her phone. She listens and then talks fast.

> DORIS
>
> Harvey? Don't hang up.
> No . . . please. I know I did a
> terrible thing but . . .

She pauses as LOUD SQUAWKS come from the other end of the line. She looks out the window and sighs.

> DORIS (Cont'd)
>
> Kissing the pool boy was no big deal.
> I didn't have the cash to tip him.

Another SQUAWK. Doris opens the window, sticks her head out and waves.

A young man cleaning the pool below waves back and throws her a kiss. Doris looks pleased.

> DORIS (Cont'd)
>
> You were so busy ogling Brenda,
> I didn't think you'd notice!

More SQUAWKS. Doris leans out the window and takes her top off. The man grins and falls into the pool.

> DORIS (Cont'd)
>
> But snuggle bunny, we need Paris!
> You've been working so hard and
> I've been so lonely! I've bought a
> ton of new lingerie!

There are no more squawks. Doris smiles the smile of victory, walks to the door, and lets in the soaking wet pool boy.

We've added some more visual interest to the shot here by moving away from the static shot of Doris simply talking on the phone. We could have also added visual interest (and lost the pool boy) by including the person on the other end of the line. The intercutting between the two conversations in two separate locations creates movement. I know that you're probably thinking that adding another location and character is a direct contradiction of what I've already told you. In this case, however, the story centers around the relationship between two characters, and so the second character has been seen in the film already and/or will appear in the rest of the film too.

You can use a location where we've already seen the second character, or you can use one that adds depth and scope to the character. In the following example, I used a massage room to indicate that here's a guy who likes to pamper himself and expects to be taken care of.

INT. BEDROOM – DAY

Doris, wearing a skimpy leopard bikini and 6-inch Lucite heels is stretched out on a window seat dialing her phone. She listens and then talks fast.

> DORIS
>
> Harvey? Don't hang up.
> No . . . please. I know I did a
> terrible thing but . . .

INT. MASSAGE ROOM – SAME

Harvey is lying face up on a massage table, draped in a white sheet, his cell phone in his hand, while a gorgeous masseuse rubs his feet.

> HARVEY
>
> Terrible is too good a word!
> Medusa! Succubus! Miley Cyrus!

Intercut Phone Conversation

> DORIS
>
> Kissing the pool boy was no big deal.
> I didn't have the cash to tip him.

> HARVEY
>
> Cash? What happened to the 20 grand
> from last week? Are you telling me
> you're so strapped you've got to
> stick your tongue

> HARVEY (Cont'd)
>
> down the throat of some chlorinated callow ramrod to spare a sawbuck?
>
> DORIS
>
> You were so busy ogling Brenda, I didn't think you'd notice.
>
> HARVEY
>
> Everyone noticed. Your ruined my birthday and you're ruining my life. I'm not so sure about Paris now.
>
> DORIS
>
> But snuggle bunny, we need Paris! You've been working so hard and I've been so lonely! I've bought a ton of new lingerie!
>
> Harvey grins and licks his lips.
>
> HARVEY
>
> Really? What color? And what about the shoes? Did you get those shoes?

We can also stoke the visuals by including some action for each character. Doris can still wave at her pool boy, and Harvey can be doing some business with his masseuse (leg lifting, slapping her arm away, screaming in pain or pleasure).

In any case, you've got to make sure that your phone conversations are interesting, visual, and important to the story.

Choreography

The same is true for shot orchestration or choreography. If you write specific choreography in your scenes (with the exception of chase, dance, or fight choreography), you'll help yourself later in the shooting process. Because the script is a shooting blueprint, careful orchestration of movement can really stand you in good stead. For example, a student wrote a scene where characters keep appearing from doors on either side of a long hallway. Their appearances were sporadic and important to be timed to coincide with certain events taking place at one end of the hall. The student initially wrote the scene this way:

INT. HALLWAY – DAY

> A long hallway lined with doors. Every few seconds, heads would pop out of each door and then quickly retreat.

Instead of writing that, I encouraged the student to make the scene seem more exciting and specific by actually describing each character's pop-out as connected with the other pop-outs to make shooting much easier and take less time. By writing the scene specifically, a kind of shot list was already in place.

INT. HALLWAY – DAY

> A long hallway with two doors on either side. Helen pops her head out of door one and quickly withdraws it just as Ben pops his head out of door three. Just as he withdraws it, Ira pops his head out of door two and then withdraws it a little before Stella pops her head out of door four.

Now it's clear what the order of popping is. Because it's all figured out beforehand, there is no need to take time during shooting to figure this out.

As I mentioned earlier, beware of writing too much description of an actual fight. Your fight choreographer will figure that out so you don't need to describe punches or specific moves.

Character Descriptions

Be careful not to describe your characters too exactly unless it's important. For example, if your character has to be blond, okay. But otherwise, hair and eye color should not be included. The same is true for body type and costume. You need to generalize. You do have to describe the person to give wardrobe hints where it is essential. For example, if your character is a Goth drummer you might write something like:

> ERIC, 20, mohawk, chains, fake leathers, and tats, is pummeling his drum set.
>
> NYLA, 17, shaved head, black lips, and mesh clothes, is staring at him with the hunger of a starving lioness.

We now get what these two are into. But you certainly don't need this:

> BRENDA, 17, dressed in a white shirt, black slacks, and a red vest, is behind a desk holding a steno pad.

Do we really care what Brenda is wearing? Not specifically. As a character point . . . if she's a naughty secretary, you might say:

> BRENDA, late 20s, dressed like a Vegas hooker trying to look legit—white shirt provocatively unbuttoned, too-big hair, and chandelier earrings, leans forward over her desk and flashes her cleavage while she licks her glossy lips.

Brenda might set the office tone and she might be "important" in the story if we need her to have an affair with the hero or the boss. But if she's just a casual character we won't see again but need her to perhaps stop our main character from entering the office, we can simply say:

BRENDA, 30s, tight lipped and dressed like a business commando, is sitting ramrod straight behind the front desk.

You can work out your business attire with wardrobe later. It usually means a dark suit but will be simple and telegraph the message you want to send regarding the office and the scene.

If you can give your descriptions this kind of flavor you'll provide an interesting read of your script and at the same time give the subtext you want for that particular scene. It's better to write descriptions that indicate character than strictly wardrobe and appearance, particularly for your main characters. This will give your actors more to work with as well.

Just in the description, the characters can understand attitude without having to wait for the dialogue. This is another way of making your script more visual. Sometimes you don't even need dialogue to make your point.

For example, in the scene with the drummer and Nyla, you could simply have the drumming stop, the drummer get down from the bandstand, grab Nyla, and give her a big sloppy kiss after which she slaps him.

```
                    ERIC
          I thought this was what you wanted.

                    NYLA
          Not my idea of foreplay!
```

Isn't that better than:

Eric stops drumming, walks down from the bandstand, and approaches Nyla.

```
                    ERIC
          Hi. I noticed you looking at me.

                    NYLA
          So. There was nothing else to look at.

                    ERIC
          But the way you were look-
          ing . . . well, it told me.

                    NYLA
          What? I don't do sign language.
```

```
                    ERIC
    No, but I do.
```

He grabs her and kisses her.

If you do that it extends the scene unnecessarily when you are looking for space to do other things. You can get to the point faster. These two feisty people are going to have a powder keg romance, and we might as well start with the explosion!

Too much time in short films is taken up by setting up scenes and situations, and all that setup might be unnecessary to the point you're making. Get to it! Sometimes you do need transitions and longer scenes to make things flow. I'm not saying that every scene needs to be short and punchy. It depends on your story and how you're playing it out.

Take that abortion scene in *Juno* that we highlighted earlier. You could omit the inside of the abortion clinic and just have her see Su-Chin's sign, say nothing, and leave right there, but we need to see her character and bravery and the idea that she has had mental issues in the past. You can still use that in a short version of *Juno* (we'll tackle that later), but you need the scene even though it takes more time, just as you need the transition fingernail scene in the clinic.

You have to decide what's important to set up and what isn't, and sometimes that means you might have to write long and then cut. But if your outline is very detailed, you won't have to struggle with cutting for length. This can get downright impossible. Once again I'm harping on the fact that you have to ask yourself every time you write a scene if it is really necessary to the story. Every scene and every bit of dialogue must serve that story in a short script.

7
BUDGET TOURNIQUETS

Stop the bleeding! Unless the script is written with production in mind, so many changes will need to be made during shooting that you'll find yourself in a living nightmare. As we've already come to see, it's better to think of technical logistics before and during writing.

To do that many screenwriters have to overcome our fear of technology. We're afraid because there are so many buttons, nobs, and things that can go wrong. The solution to all of this is simple. Partner up with someone who likes gadgets. And if you can't do that, then get yourself equipment that is laughingly simple (iPhones, iPads, point and shoot cameras), and learn to use it. Not every film (especially if intended for online viewing) needs to be shot with a Red camera.

More mundane cameras may have what we might consider quality drawbacks (purists whine that the quality isn't as good as film, etc.), but forget about that. If the important thing is the message and what you want to get across, then be willing to back away from some of the things you think are quality essentials. Once again, if the story is compelling, people will forgive the odd technical glitch. You just have to make sure it can be heard well (sound is paramount) and actually seen . . . not too dark or too light.

So let's say that you've written a perfect shoot-friendly short about five to seven minutes long. You've told a simple story using a few characters and a few locations. You've used effective visuals, and you've been innovative with production design. But in spite of all of that, be aware that there are some things you simply can't do without in the shooting process. You need to figure out how to make these things financially viable by coming up with ways to stop your budget from bleeding while you shoot. There are ways of doing that in pre-production.

Here Are Some Things to Think About

Let's say you have $4,000 to spend (the average price of a five- to seven-minute movie done without having to rent camera equipment; rentals will up that by a few thousand). That $4,000 includes catering; renting a generator or electricity on set; an equipment truck to haul lights, cameras, props, etc., to locations; hair and makeup costs; wardrobe; some post costs; hard drive costs; camera cards; permits; and so on.

Here Are Areas Where You Might Save

Crew and Actors

Let's assume you can get actors for free (you usually can by putting ads in the casting magazines) because they need footage for their reels. You can also get interns/students/relatives and friends to work as free crew. Keep in mind that relationships may be strained during the stress of filming. Remember to treat everyone with respect and kindness—especially if they are working for free. That means you should NOT work your crew more than 12 hours . . . and that's a lot. Many student filmmakers make the mistake of holding punishing working hours because they haven't prepared well, are indecisive, make mistakes, or are just plain ruthless. If you can't do it in 12 hours, extend your shooting schedule. This will cost you a little more money but it will be worth it to save your crew and actors from hating you. A five- to seven-minute film takes about three and a half days to shoot, counting half a day for pickups.

Equipment

If you're a student, you can use school equipment for free. Cash problems arise when students try to get fancy and want to rent dollies, steady-cams, and other high-end stuff they think they need to make their production pop. And there's the old horror of wanting to shoot on film instead of digitally. I tell those people to get over themselves! You don't need fancy equipment to make a really good film. So consider some ways you can save on equipment.

Camera

If you already have a camera and tripod, you're ahead. If not, try to borrow these or use a cinematographer who already has them and is willing to work for free to complete his or her reel. And remember the less sophisticated options. The feature *Tangerine* was shot on an iPhone 5s!

Lights

You could shoot with available light (a little risky) and outdoors. You'll be ahead. Of course, if you rent a camera and lights, you'll be out significant money. Students can use school equipment.

Permits

Permits are an expensive necessity in most cities, but you can certainly choose locations where the permits are cheaper. You can also shoot in places that may not require them, but be careful: A permit will protect you as well as property owners. It's not a good idea to shoot without them or to try and cheat by stealing shots in locations requiring them. It's not worth risking serious trouble to save permit money!

Location Costs

Find locations that you can borrow. Use your friends and relatives to help you use their properties for free—houses, apartments, even offices can be "borrowed" from amenable contacts. Just make sure that you clean up after yourself and don't cause any damage. That means you'll have to get insurance.

Insurance

A real necessity. If you're a student, the school usually takes care of that (not all schools do), but if not, then there are companies that will provide insurance coverage by the day at a fairly reasonable rate.

Generator

While it's true that you don't want to blow someone's electrical system when you shoot interiors with lights (a generator could end up costing you as much as $200 for the shoot or as little as $45; size matters here so see what you can find), you might not always need one. Some schools actually forbid the use of generators for safety concerns. To get around the generator issue you can, as professor and filmmaker Mick Hurbis (CUNY) says: "Use daylight with bounced light and you can scout locations for electrical loads. Use locations that can handle the lights you require. Especially now with high sensitivity CMOS sensors and low wattage LED lights, the need for a generator is greatly reduced. Generators require specialized crew and time."

Hair and Makeup

A makeup kit will cost you $50.00. To find a makeup artist, go to beauty schools and see if you can get an aspiring wannabe for free. Lots of people are looking to work on small films to build up their experience and set cred. If you need elaborate makeup (scars, horror faces, etc.) you may have to pay extra. Make sure you negotiate but not so hard that you alienate a potential makeup contact.

Truck Rental

Depending on the amount of equipment you are planning to use, you'll definitely need one of these. Some people make do with a flotilla of cars (their own and friends) or a U-Haul, but frankly a truck equipped with racks and a really good lift is preferable. It will make your life so much easier so you might want to spring for the $450 it might cost you for a three-day shoot. And you'll have to count in gas. If you're shooting in one location, you may not need a truck at all.

Food for Cast and Crew

You are going to have to feed your crew and actors—especially if they are working for free. DO NOT SKIMP ON FOOD! This means that three days of meals (three meals a day and snacks) may cost you $1,000. If you have generous family (a mom or sister who cooks), you can cut down on your costs. But this is really where lots of your budget will go.

Production Design

Be careful that your sets are not so elaborate that they will run you into serious money. Find innovative and energetic production designers at the beginning of their careers. And make sure they come to you with lots of ideas. It is possible to cheat lots of locations with production design. Remember my earlier examples of the submarine and the jail cell? Be creative. Things don't have to be real if they can appear real! Just make sure that the cheat translates well in the shot. Test to make sure because there's nothing worse than having something look great in person but laughable on screen.

Props

Make use of stuff you, your family, or friends have lying around. If you can't do that, you'll have to rent props from a prop house. Many of these have student rates. If you're not a student, carefully consider what you'll really need. Weapons will cost you extra even if they are fake.

Cops

Even if weapons (guns in particular) are fake, if you take them outside, you'll have to rent an off-duty cop to be present on set, and you'll also have to inform police. These days it's too dangerous to be out in the open with weapons of any kind, even if they are innocent and fake. And this is also true of shooting indoors. Make sure that you alert the police about your intended use of a gun (even a fake one) during your shoot. If you don't, you may be in for trouble.

That's what happened to a film crew in Los Angeles on August 3, 2013. As reported in the *Los Angeles Times*, the students were using fake guns to shoot a robbery scene in a suburban coffee shop when an alarmed bystander thought it was the real thing and called 911. Police arrived to find one man holding what looked like an AR-15 and another one carrying what looked like a handgun. Both were wearing hooded sweatshirts and masks.

A police captain told the *Times* the man with the rifle dropped his weapon immediately, but the man with the handgun hesitated. Police audio obtained by KTLA-TV revealed an officer shouting, "Drop the gun! Drop it, drop it, drop it." That student was almost shot. Close call. Be very cautious!

Costumes

If you're shooting in present day you can sometimes get the actors to supply their own clothing. Just keep in mind that things might get damaged so if you're supplying clothing you might have to double up. The most common doubling-up items are T shirts and shirts. Usually, though, actor-supplied clothing will work. If you need to use uniforms you've got money issues. People who wear uniforms in your script need to be kept to a minimum. If, for example, you've got a murder scene with lots of cops around, you'll have to spring for those outfits. A better solution might be just to have one cop and the rest plainclothes detectives. Another way of cutting down would be to get the CSI folks to wear paper coveralls (they do that on British crime dramas all the time). Those are cheap to buy and can save you lots of money. If you've got military in your script, the same holds true. Try to cut down on the extras and main characters because combat outfits will run up your budget drastically. Same is true for the guns they carry (as we've already seen).

Stunt People

If you have any kind of stunts in your movie, you'll have to engage a stunt coordinator who will supply you with stunt people. Sometimes you can get stunt coordinators for a very low price (maybe even free) if they are just starting out. What you don't want to do is have elaborate stunts that can actually hurt people! And, as mentioned before, sometimes even simple "stunts" like head bumping or falling might need stunt people.

Fight Choreographer

If you have a fight sequence in your movie you will need to get a fight choreographer or else the fight will look fake. Some filmmakers believe they can actually direct fight sequences to look authentic, but the results don't play that out. You need someone who can make your fight look as effective as possible, and to do that you need someone who's an expert. Sometimes these people will work for free too.

You can see how your budget can bleed. But you can be smart and save yourself. What follows is a case study where a filmmaker was smart and made a lovely little film for an astounding $50.00. She became a budget super hero for doing that!

CASE STUDY

The project was made for the Hollywood Black Film Festival Mobile Competition and Indi.com (it was based on votes). The challenge was to create a superhero-themed story. The filmmaker (my student Ebony Gilbert) decided to explore what a superhero meant and how the people in our lives embody that. She decided to showcase the everyday life of a single mother and to highlight that woman's strength through the eyes of her superhero-obsessed child.

Remember, she was able to make the five-minute film for $50. Here's how:

Camera

A cell phone—the iPhone 5s.

Sound

Her script used only voiceover. This was also recorded on the cell phone. In a quiet room she had her actress speak into the phone in the video recording mode. This was done before she shot any of the scenes.

Editing

She used Final Cut to edit and did it herself.

Lighting

She decided to do the film in black and white to cover up any lighting problems. She says, "We just used God's beautiful natural light (lol) and every lamp we had at home!"

Locations

- A city street shot in her neighborhood.
- A city bus: shot on an actual bus ride—unobtrusive because of the cell phone use.

Both those scenes took an hour to shoot.
- An apartment (the primary location): her own. This avoided paying to use a space.

The night before the shoot she blocked off where she wanted to shoot and where she would place the camera and the lights and marked it with duct tape on the floor. In black marker she wrote on the tape each scene number, for example, (S1) for scene number one.

Casting

She did not want to use more than two actors since she wanted it to be character focused and simple to shoot. She promoted the audition via social media and held an audition at her church's facility during one of their big casting calls for another project. She contacted the theater director at the church.

Crew

The crew included the filmmaker as the writer, director, editor, and producer. Her brother acted as director of photography, and her mother worked as the production assistant and casting coordinator.

Budget

The budget was a little less than 50 bucks and included props (superhero items), food for cast and crew, and gas reimbursement.

The film, a moving and a lovely little tribute to working single moms everywhere, made industry folks take notice of Ebony Gilbert, a talented and production-savvy screenwriter!

To summarize, if you want to eliminate budget bleeds:

1. Shoot locally.
2. Limit your locations and borrow them.

3. Where possible, shoot outdoors.
4. Use colleagues, friends, family, interns as crew.
5. Don't work your crew more than 12 hours a day.
6. Forgo, if possible, elaborate or unusual costumes and uniforms.
7. Try to cut down your shooting days without rushing to get your work done. Make sure you rehearse. That will make your shooting easier.
8. Create a comprehensive shot list *before* you get on set.
9. Make sure you get lots of coverage.
10. Plan for an extra half-day for pick-ups if you do miss something.
11. Shoot your most complicated/difficult scene first so you'll get that out of the way. Filmmakers starting out usually take far too long to shoot small scenes when they first get started and then have to rush like crazy to get their large scenes finished at the end of the shoot.

8

THE SHOOTING SCRIPT

It may be that in the interpretation of the script, a plethora of angles will be necessary to create the desired effect of a scene. That's why the initial writing of the script needs to be angle free but mood and effect specific, as we've already seen in Chapter 4. Because you may not be entirely aware of all the cinematic possibilities inherent in the scene until you talk with the cinematographer, it's necessary to avoid including angles in the initial script to facilitate a better read for everyone involved in the production.

That literary read will make it easier to raise funds, cast actors, and inform other crew members. When you finally get down to pre-production planning, however, you're going to need to know what cameras you'll need; how you want to light; and what props, stunts, production design, and sound work you'll need.

In order to do that you'll need to create a shooting script that reveals those things to your crew. That's why all sounds, significant props, and stunts need to be written in capital letters. If costumes are vital to a scene, you might want to write these in caps as well. And ultimately, you may want to include actual angles.

First, you'll need to number the scenes. These numbers will help you communicate to your crew which scenes you're talking about instead of referring to story points. These numbers will also help you when you create the shooting schedule. While we're on that, here are a few points about creating a viable shooting schedule.

Take note of your day and night indicators. If these indicators are used in interior locations, you don't have to worry about them because lighting (or lack of it) can cheat time of day. However, if your time-of-day indicators are in exterior locations, you'll have to plan your shooting schedule accordingly. This is also true of location indicators. If your film includes a warehouse, for example, all those scenes will be shot in one day even though they may be scattered throughout the script. In these cases, because scripts are not shot in sequence, your scene numbers will help you arrange your shots together to accommodate night or day or locations.

Creating Shot Lists

If you are directing the film, you need to come up with lists of shots that you'll use.

Now let's get back to angles. Remember our chef scene in Chapter 4? Here's part of it again:

> TOM, 26, wearing a chef's uniform bursting at the seams, stands in front of a grimy, state-of-the-art stove, cutting a stick of butter into a frying pan. Still holding the butter, he picks up a slice of bread but drops it on the floor. As he stoops to pick it up, he drops the butter, slips, falls, and hits his head on the oven door handle.

We've already discussed how the way this is written indicates possible shots. Looking at this scene again, we can get more specific when we create our shot list because clear clues exist in the body of the description.

Here's a sample initial shot list:

- Medium Wide on Tom (to include stove)
- Close as he cuts butter into frying pan.

- Widen as he picks up slice of bread.
- Wider as he drops it on the floor.
- Close on bread on floor.
- Widen as he stoops to pick it up.
- Closer as he drops butter.
- Widen as he slips on butter, falls, and hits his head.

Added coverage:

- Widen as he drops bread on floor and stoops to pick it up.
- Close on butter.
- Close on head hitting.
- Wide on entire sequence as he drops, picks up, and hits head.

This shot list is very detailed, provides lots of coverage, and will take a significant amount of time to shoot. You may not have the time or inclination to shoot this much. Discuss the list with your Director of Photography (DP) to come up with something that is workable for both of you.

The shot list will accompany the script—you can write your shots in the margin (that is, line the script with shots) initially as you make these decisions with your cinematographer. You can also write your preferred angles into your script and, just in case, keep your coverage angles separate. You may want to do both.

> CLOSE ON TOM, 26, wearing A CHEF'S UNIFORM BURSTING AT THE SEAMS (WIDEN TO MEDIUM), stands in front of a grimy state-of-the-art stove cutting a stick of butter into a frying pan. Still holding the butter, he picks up a slice of bread (TIGHTENING SLIGHTLY) as he drops it on the floor (CU BREAD ON FLOOR). WIDEN as he drops the butter and WIDEN MORE as he slips, falls, and hits his head on the oven door handle.

I don't think all this rewriting is necessary. It's so much easier to just insert the shots into the existing script. The places where the shots are inserted can act as editing points later. You probably have noticed how many shot options present themselves when shooting even this short snippet of a scene. If you've written it the way you've seen it in your mind, that's not your worry (unless you're directing the piece). If you are NOT directing the piece and the director wants you to generate a shooting script (not always the case with short films although it could happen), you simply need to follow the director's instructions regarding angles to create the scene as written and work with that person to create an angle-inclusive shooting script if that is required.

Story Boards

Many short films just use story boards. These are drawings (can be crudely drawn) in sequence with some directions and dialogue playing out your entire film. You could draw these yourself or get a really good story board person to do that. These will help you visualize the movie in detail.

Pre-Production Script Changes

If you're a screenwriter directing your script for the first time, you need to first learn as much as you can about the directing process. This is NOT a book about directing. To learn how to make that transition, you should read books, take courses, shadow other directors and, above all, ask for help and advice from people who've had experience. And that doesn't just mean directing experience. You can benefit greatly from the advice of all sorts of talented people who have worked on other movies. DPs, production designers, gaffers, sound people, costumers, actors can all help you to make your movie better.

Taking that advice usually changes the shooting script—sometimes drastically. Don't be daunted by this. These changes may be things you didn't realize when you were writing the script even though you had production in mind. When it comes to the actual shooting script, things always change according to the exigencies of the film making process and these changes are necessary to make your movie great.

I learned that from the mistakes I made directing my first project. I'd been hired by a network to direct a film that would air as part of a series. In the crazy fog of youth, I didn't imagine that any mistakes I made would appear on national television for everybody to notice. I foolishly believed I wouldn't make any mistakes. Boy was I wrong.

Hard-headed as only a 23 year old can be, I spent a long time lining up a wide shot with my DP and insisting we use it as an establishing. I didn't listen to him when he suggested that the shot was too wide and the details I was looking for wouldn't be seen. He was right. On screen the effect I was going for was lost in the space. ARGH!

There were many more instances like that on this particular shoot and I won't punish either of us by describing them, but I learned from that. Take the suggestions of your DP! That doesn't mean the DP can take over the shoot (that happened to me once, where I yelled cut and the DP didn't cut, so I fired him and got one that would listen). It does mean that you have to consider everything carefully and put your prima donna hat away.

Crew

Along with DPs, here are some other people on your crew that can help you.

Gaffers

Find people who really know lighting and can make your movie look great. And make sure that your gaffer and your

DP work well together. These two people are essential to helping you get your vision across. Make sure you discuss the mood you are looking for and the effect you want your film to have with the person who can deliver those things. I know lots of first time film makers who've insisted on shooting with very low light against the advice of their DPs and Gaffers and ended up with something that could barely be seen on the big screen. Remember, just because you can see in an editing bay doesn't mean that it will translate to a large size when you project.

Production Designers

Make sure that you find production designers who will tell you the truth about what's possible. If you're building sets, get people who know how to do that and will rein you in when you want to attempt the impossible. If you want to build a boxing ring on a sound stage (as one of my students did) make sure that your production designer lets you know the costs involved and the time it will take to build that set. One of our students actually built a pirate ship on the sound stage and spent many thousands of dollars doing that. They had the money but the final movie didn't really justify the cost or the time and trouble. Make certain that your production designer knows how to cut corners and give you a look that will make your movie shine without costing you big bucks.

Actors

Input from actors is huge, particularly when it comes to dialogue. I always advise my students to use their most difficult and engaging scenes to audition actors. If they can do those well, you're pretty certain they can do the easy ones too. And I recommend rehearsing with your actors to get the dialogue right.

When actors get dialogue they quickly find those places where the words just don't work. Take their advice and change the dialogue to make it work! Woody Allen constantly tells his actors that if they don't like the dialogue he's written they can change it. An actor who is uncomfortable with what he's saying won't come across the way you want him too. Again, that doesn't mean actors can take over the movie by throwing out the dialogue you wrote. Have reasonable discussions with them and help them to make their speeches more comfortable and you'll strengthen your working relationship and also strengthen your script.

Making the transition from screenwriter to director isn't easy. It takes guts and confidence. Learn as much as you can beforehand and take the plunge. Expect to make mistakes. But minimize them by surrounding yourself with people who know more than you do, are excited about your project and believe in you. Don't be afraid to ask for their help in all things. They will respect you for it and feel that they have even more of a stake in the movie than if they just followed orders. Remember: Film-making is a collaborative art!

9

YOUR TYPE

The Feature-Based Short

As an earlier chapter pointed out, your short film is a calling card that will help you get noticed by the industry, but it can also be used as a "sizzle reel" of sorts to sell that feature you want to make. It can help you raise money by demonstrating your film's value. We'll discuss how this works with fundraising in Chapter 10, but basically what it means is that your short film will need to demonstrate a compelling theme. It should also introduce people to your characters and demonstrate your writing style, your ability to handle dialogue, and your talent for creating tension and conflict—in short your filmmaking charisma that will all be evident in your feature script and, later, in the feature itself.

When you take your short to film festivals, it's important to make "buyers" realize that it's only the first step in your burgeoning career. Too many filmmakers never get traction because, even though they might get interest in their short, when someone asks them to talk about what their next step is, they shrug. It would be much better if they could pull out a feature script based on their short and describe their intent to get that made. People who haven't done that have related many sad stories indeed. For example, a student of mine—a brilliant director—got a talented writer to provide a script and made a fabulous short film that got play in lots of festivals. He was ultimately approached by a major studio who promised him a directing deal if he could come up with a feature script based on the short. Unfortunately, because he wasn't a writer and not attached to the script, he was unable to do that and the directing deal fell through. Today he's out of the industry and all that talent went to waste. The writer went on to have a significant career.

Make sure that you are attached to the script you write for your short (at least a co-writing credit). That way, if they want the script/story you can at least hold on to some kind of involvement. Another student who wanted to direct wrote the script for his short, and a major studio liked it so much it paid him for the feature script he had to go along with it and let him direct—for a few days. They threw him off the picture and hired a major director, but at least he had a writing credit and launched a successful screenwriting career. I've left out the names of these ex-students to protect them, but their stories are not atypical. This happens all the time.

It's important to understand that people are looking for original voices and stories, and you've got to demonstrate that in any way you can. If you are able to direct your own short screenplay, you should definitely do that. If you aren't confident in directing, then work with a co-director. In any case, even if you get someone else to direct, make sure that you have a feature script you've written to go along with the short. Chances are the director will be overlooked and the screenplay acquired!

So how do you squeeze a feature-length script into a short? You don't. A short is a different animal. The idea is to give buyers a taste of your abilities—a taste of the short—a teaser of what they can expect to see more of in a feature. Keep in mind that a short must stand alone or it won't get festival play. It isn't enough just to shoot a trailer (we'll discuss this later) or a couple of scenes. You've got to have a beginning, middle, and end.

That means that the short won't have all the elements of the feature and the story will not be complete. What it should include is the main characters, the essence of the story (what it's really about), and some significant aspects of the story. And don't forget, it should demonstrate your particular sensibility and style regarding visuals, dialogue, action, etc.

How do you decide what elements of the feature to put into a short? To show you what to do, I'll break down the movie *Juno*, from the Academy Award–winning screenplay by Diablo Cody, by putting it into an outline format (first introduced in Chapter 4). Then I'll show you the possibilities of getting a short out of that film.

Remember, each plot point takes about five minutes, though some can be more or less. Here's the outline for Juno. It's a 90-minute film, so the 24-point outline structure will be altered slightly. The first act ends much earlier (page 25—plot point 4—or can even be considered at plot point 3—pages 15 to 20), the midpoint will be plot point 9 (pages 45 to 50), and Act Three will begin at plot point 15 (pages 75 to 80). Spikes may not be relevant.

ACT ONE

Credits: We meet Juno, she tells us about her sexual encounter, and we get her attitude. That takes four minutes. The actual movie begins as she picks up a pregnancy test.

1. She picks up a pregnancy test. It's positive. (In a 90-page script like this, you could consider this the "hook.") She goes home (more character revelation here with licorice, her room décor, and her telephone—a hamburger). She calls her friend and

tells her. She introduces us to Bleeker, the high school runner who is the "father."
2. She tells him she's pregnant and discusses abortion. We see both of them at school and their relationship with each other and other students. She goes home and calls Women Now to make an abortion appointment. We learn she is 16.
3. We are introduced to her parents and find out her relationship with them.
    She goes to the abortion clinic but she leaves. She tells her friend she's staying pregnant and will give the baby up. Her friend suggests looking for adoptive parents in the Penny Saver. We can look at this as the end of Act One (p. 20), setting us up for finding the adoptive parents and seeing what ensues.

ACT TWO

4. Her friend suggests looking for adoptive parents in the Penny Saver. They find a couple.
    Meanwhile we learn that Bleeker's mom doesn't like Juno. And then Juno tells her parents she's pregnant and that she is going to give the baby to a couple she found on the Penny Saver. The parents react. She invites her dad to meet the couple with her.
5. Juno and her dad meet the adoptive couple and their lawyer. Juno says she wants a closed adoption. We find out the woman (Vanessa) is desperate for a child.
6. On a trip upstairs to the bathroom, Juno snoops around and discovers the husband is a musician. He appears, and they bond over guitars. The wife finds this upsetting and gets them back downstairs where she asks how serious Juno is about the adoption. Juno tells her she is definite about giving the child to them. Vanessa is thrilled as Juno and her dad leave.

7. More of Bleeker. Juno's ultrasound. Juno's stepmom chews out the technician in favor of single motherhood. Juno visits Marc and Vanessa to show them the ultrasound. She and Marc bond even more. Vanessa comes home and things get uncomfortable. Juno's mom talks to her about boundaries.
8. Vanessa visits Bleeker and talks about adoption. It's awkward. Marc and Vanessa have awkwardness of their own over the baby's room. Juno runs into Vanessa at the mall and sees how desperate Vanessa is for motherhood.
9. **MIDPOINT**
Juno and Bleeker fall out. Juno visits Marc and he comes on to her subtly. He tells her he's going to divorce Vanessa. She tries to talk him out of it.
10. Vanessa comes home, and Marc tells her he's not ready to be a father. She is devastated. They fight in front of Juno, who leaves and breaks down.
11. Marc calls a lawyer to arrange for the divorce. Juno leaves a note at their house. Juno and her dad have a talk about love and relationships.
12. Juno fills Bleeker's mailbox with Tic Tacs and tells him she loves him. They make up.
13. Juno goes into labor.
14. Juno has the baby.
End of Act Two.

ACT THREE

15. Dad comforts Juno. Bleeker shows up.
16. Vanessa bonds with baby.
17. Bleeker and Juno go on with their lives.

You will notice when you watch this film that some of the plot points are very short and others go on longer. This is usual.

So now we're ready to come up with a short film inspired by/based on *Juno*. The first thing that needs to be done is to determine what this film is *really about*. If this was your film, what would you want to let people know you're ultimately saying in your feature? At the same time, you'd want to introduce them to the characters and the sensibility of the film. Because you don't have much time, you need to make sure you don't include too much but that you show enough so people "get it." You'll also want to make people curious—you want to make them want to see more of the story . . . maybe even the rest of the story. But you also want to make sure that the short stands alone.

In *Juno*'s case, we can determine that the film is saying that abortion is not necessarily a good solution to teenage pregnancy.

Because you want your short to be shown at film festivals, you need to make sure that your film is no longer than 15 minutes. Twelve minutes would be ideal, so let's see how we can make this work in this case.

When you look at the outline, you first have to determine what the subplot is and how important it is to your central story. Juno has a couple of subplots. The main subplot is the relationship between Marc and Vanessa, and although this is crucial to the later story, it doesn't really contribute to the major thrust of what we are saying in our film. Another subplot is the relationship between Juno and her parents and Juno's relationship with Bleeker. Again, although vital, these subplots don't apply to our essential theme.

Looking at the feature outline, we can determine that our short could easily and effectively take place by just adapting the first act of the movie. Remember that because we don't want to simply lift the first act out of the feature and plop it into a short, we'll have to make some adjustments to make it effective. So let's see how we can do that by outlining the short.

Let's say we want to make it 10 minutes long. As per that outline from Chapter 4:

Act 1:   pages 1 to 3
Act 2:   pages 4 to 8
Act 3:   pages 9 to 10

So with a *Juno* short we can do this:

Act One: Short Version

Page 1:   Juno and Bleeker have sex in a chair.
Page 2:   Juno goes for a pregnancy test. It's positive.
Page 3:   Discussion with a friend. She will go to a clinic.

Act Two: Short Version

Page 4:   She shows up at the clinic. Meets school friend. "Fingernails."
Page 5:   Runs from the clinic and tells friend she will keep the kid.
Page 6:   They look in the Penny Saver and find a couple.
Page 7:   She tells her parents.
Page 8:   She tells Bleeker she's giving it up.

Act Three: Short Version

Page 9:   She has the baby.
Page 10:   She cries while cuddling with Bleeker.

The couple is left out of this on purpose but is "teased" in the Penny Saver ad. That can come out later in the feature. But you can see how if you shorten some of the existing scenes (i.e., in the "fingernails" scene with her friend, etc.) we can get it into 10 pages easily.

If you want to include the couple, you can play with this and make the film another few minutes longer.

Exercise

Watch *Juno* and see if you can create outlines for a 12-, 15-, and even 5-minute movie.

This will help you see how you can break down your own feature and decide how to create a short based on it!

The Editing Showcase Short

Some of you might want to make a short to provide yourself with a sample of how well you can edit. If you want to do that, you are going to need to write a movie with thematically significant cuts. That means you'll want to get into the action adventure genre or be experimental. But you'll need to temper those models with stories that demonstrate your practical editing skills by working with dialogue, character movement, location exploration, and relationship between action and dialogue.

Don't make the mistake of thinking that showcasing your editing skills means constant quick and flashy sequences. And remember, the editing must blend seamlessly with the film. Don't write in cuts just for their own sake. Make sure that your story holds together and that the editing contributes to it rather than detracts.

The Cinematography Showcase Short

I get lots of wannabe cinematographers who want to make shorts to show off their camera skills. Unfortunately, most of them give little thought to story and substance. A film should be much more than just a series of beautiful shots. You need to write it so it's visually exciting but also has subtext and emotion that will involve audiences. People will only look at pretty pictures for so long. You need to give them a reason to keep watching. And you can do that by making your cinematography work with your characterization. Actors love close-ups, and if you can concentrate on aspects of character business in the script that will be revealed through adroit cinematography, you've hit the mark.

Remember also to vary your style to show how you can shoot in different arenas. That means you might want to write a variety of scenes with different textures (gritty, bucolic, etc.) and different lighting requirements. But again, make sure that these arenas and textures are integral to your story. Otherwise, the film will fall apart and will not serve your interests.

The Production Design Showcase Short

Production design is tough on a low budget. It takes ingenuity, creative imagination, and craft skills to pull off believable design on a shoestring. But it is possible. In order to do that, you've got to make sure that your story is simple and direct, that it has perhaps only one location, and that it can be shot tightly to minimize and limit paraphernalia.

One of my students wanted to create a prison environment for her jailhouse short. She couldn't get permission to shoot in a prison (nearly impossible for student productions), and she had no money for iron bars, so she glued paper towel rolls together, painted them and propped them up to make those "bars". It worked because it was done with painstaking care and because her cinematographer was able to shoot in a way that didn't reveal the cheat.

Another student wrote a short about a young child who found a magical cave that included an artisan workshop. She shot tightly in a room filled with bric-a-brac and a jumble of interesting objects she obtained from thrift stores. The place looked incredible and because the story centered on the boy and not the objects themselves, her background looks fabulous. Even in production design showcase shorts it's important to understand that the design creates the environment in which the characters operate and that the characters are still the most important elements of the scene. Although production design gives color, texture, and context to the scene, it should never be the main focus unless your story is entirely about environment.

There are movies where environment is the star (fantasy and space adventures, etc.), but those are difficult to do on small budgets. One of my graduate students did make two films in which environment featured strongly. One film took place in a submarine, and he had to build that from scratch on the sound stage, including appropriate, real-looking submarine paraphernalia. His other film took place on a space station on a distant planet. Again he had to build real-looking space station paraphernalia. In both cases, the student worked diligently to do that and was successful because his shots didn't focus on the environment even though both environments were key to his story. He was able to make the audience feel the claustrophobia of the submarine and the technical jumble of the space station by keeping his shots tight and having his characters move their bodies in ways that reflected the spaces they occupied.

The shorts I've just used as examples were all shot on a sound stage where the filmmakers had the time and space to build their projects. If you don't have access to a sound stage, you can do the same thing in a garage or warehouse or other empty space, or you can carefully choose locations that will significantly contribute to your production design. Just keep in mind that some locations may be expensive and also that building your set can also be expensive. Better to write shorts where you can use props to create the design you want. Just know that props will also add considerable heft to your budget, but sometimes that's the price you have to pay to show what you can do.

Costume Design Showcase Shorts

Be prepared to do lots of sewing if you want to showcase this talent. You'll have to put in a lot of hours, and you'll also have to pony up the cost of fabrics. It's a real *Project Runway* experience if you want to demonstrate your talent for costume design. Students who have done this have usually written period pieces, but period pieces can be expensive because beyond costumes it's necessary to provide other period props.

As far as costume is concerned, you can get a lot of mileage from vintage clothes shops, but if you really want to prove you can design costumes from scratch, prepare to work your fingers to the bone. To show off in this way, you'll have to create stories where characters are "defined" by their clothes, where outfits make up part of the culture of the story. Think *Downton Abbey* or *Wings of the Dove*. Stories where class distinctions and manners are in the forefront work for these kinds of showcases, and they can be a treat for the eyes so make sure that you're working with a cinematographer who has a knack for shooting detail and enjoys a slow pace so that audiences can take in the glory of your creations.

The PSA

If you want to create public service announcements (PSAs) to advance your activist agenda or make an infomercial to sell a product, you'll need to know that it's vitally important to create some kind of viewer draw. That means your short needs to be compelling visually, but it also needs to be character driven so that audiences will take notice.

Remember that old environmental PSA that featured a Native American crying? That went over especially well because the actor's face provided compelling subtext to the piece. It's important that you try and find images that will involve the audience emotionally. For example, when I worked with students to create a PSA to accompany Participant Media's documentary *A Place at the Table* about hunger in America, we made sure that the subjects featured in our short were relatable. To make audiences realize that hungry people were not stereotypical, we featured single moms, overweight teenagers, and farmers. We showed well-dressed people "shopping" at food banks. We showed typical school kids eating meager lunches. We wanted audiences to identify with our principals in order to understand that hunger was not limited solely to the homeless and indigent. It worked. The PSA was successful and made our point, and Participant Media ran it on its website.

The Infomercial

This is really about selling something. In order to sell a product and make a successful infomercial, you need to keep the PSA "rules" in mind. There's an art in advertising for sure, as evidenced by the nature of commercials in general. People watch commercials for their entertainment value. Commercials during the Superbowl are watched with gusto. Those have huge budgets, but it is possible to create something with imagination and verve on smaller budgets if you write them energetically and with lots of thought. Be clever and compelling. Use characters people can relate to and, most of all, recognize and define a need in the audience members that they can respond to. Convince them that they can't live without your product while showing them what it does in clever and artistic ways and you'll be a success.

New Platforms

Exciting new platforms are constantly being developed, and these platforms will change the way we make movies. That change will also directly affect how we write them.

As we adopt new technologies, we need to learn how to include camera directions into our scripts without making them angle happy, and that will require some pretty interesting gymnastics on the part of the screenwriter. Take virtual reality (VR), for example. I'm currently working with some people who are developing a virtual reality project that will be incorporated into a roving museum exhibit featuring the history of a Los Angeles neighborhood. It's a project that presents definite writing and shooting challenges.

It's important to understand that when you're working in virtual reality, people will be using a device (like Google Cardboard) to look at your film. This means that in order to create a sense of virtual reality, POV (point of view) shots may be consistently required to give the audience member the feeling that he is a character in the film and thoroughly present in it at all times. That means you've got to find a way of writing the literary script that will indicate that, and when you create the shooting script you've got to work out how the movie will be shot in ways that you haven't been used to shooting. In fact, some of these ways haven't even been invented yet because people are still trying to figure out how virtual reality can work in extended storytelling.

VR scripts have to be written in different ways. For example, if the entire script is a certain character's POV, you can't introduce that character into the description because the audience will never see him. Even so, you've got to designate angles that will reflect how that character sees things. If, for example, the character is a child, your shots may be tilting up a lot of the time as the child looks at things taller than she is. If the character is climbing on objects and seeing things from a height, your shots will be tilting down. But while you're doing this, you don't want to create a script that is so angle happy it's impossible to read. It's a tough job. You've got more leeway in the shooting script, but there are ways to make the literary script more appealing.

For example:

INT. BEDROOM—DAY

> A French bulldog's face comes closer and closer, its nose twitching. It suddenly moves up and down on a blue blanket and then is swept off a bed and onto the floor. A hand reaches down and scratches it behind the ears. A DOOR CREAKS OPEN. Across the room, a tall, thin girl dressed in a Nazi uniform stomps in. A SCREAM. The blue blanket quickly moves upward. Total blackness.

You should notice that in order to get the character to look toward the door, I used a sound cue. This gives motivation for the audience member's attention to shift in that direction. Other motivators can be used—anxiety, quick head movements, jerky eye movements—all of these things can guide audiences to certain portions of the shot if the shot is wide and includes the entire room.

In the case of my example, the entire movie will be POV so we won't see things as observers but as participants. The bulldog's face moves toward the camera lens. Think of the film being shot with a GoPro where the camera operator is the actor. This can get really tricky and blurs the line between crew and actor. In fact, the camera actually becomes the actor by virtue of the angles required. If the camera is the "actor" and you want the audience to experience what that actor actually sees, then head turns, tilts, eyes shutting, etc., need to be re-created as close to a person's physical reality as possible. Pans may be swifter, things may appear out of focus, space between objects and the camera will be dictated by reality. This presents quite a series of complex issues for directors, cinematographers, and camera operators—issues that screenwriters working with these people on shooting scripts need to be ready to address.

If VR movies have audiences visiting certain spaces, then what they actually look at is no longer in the hands of the director and editor. This will drastically change the editing process and greatly influence sound design. They will also make a difference in acting techniques and in the technology of film itself.

An online article on the Unit9.com site says that script writing is becoming more like world building. "Instead of a series of events set in time, scriptwriting is more about creating a world and connecting everything with your narrative." It puts forward the scriptwriter's dilemma:

> *Three characters pointing guns at each other in a VR film called Reservoir Dogs. Does your viewer look at one of those guys but miss the shots fired by another? Or maybe viewers see only the gorgeous sweeping landscapes outside and miss the whole scene. We have to write for multiple possibilities. You can lead your viewer, you can entice him to look and you can give him a good reason to pay attention to something specific.*
> (Unit 9, 2016)

These enticements can be through sound or other action but must be startling enough to change the viewer's point of view. The article writer goes on to say that people will suggest locking the viewer's point of view (as in continuous character POV shots), but says that this breaks the fundamental reason for using VR as a storytelling medium.

That may be true; however, it's an experimental game now, and screenwriters have to come up with original ways to involve the audience in this new form of storytelling. Techies are saying that VR takes a lot from gaming but allows for a more elaborate interface. Good screenwriters aren't interested in having characters walk through a space shooting everything in their path. We're much more interested in motivation, character development, and story and that's why the new VR world is such a challenge. It forces us to make the subtle and internal somehow real in the way it's portrayed—all through an audience lens that has increasingly more and more autonomy.

No matter what the platform, the important thing to remember if you are shooting your own project is that you need to make the process as comfortable for yourself as possible. That means you should develop your own system for creating a shooting script and shot list. Just make sure your process is clear and communicable to others. There's nothing more anxiety producing on a shoot than working in a situation where the instructions are confusing, unclear, or just plain stupid. Make sure that you've discussed ad nauseam your shooting plans for the script well before you get on set. Productions fail when those in charge are unprepared and haven't done their homework.

Because new platforms are moviemaking's Wild West and there are no specific ways of writing scripts for VR projects, it's a learn-as-you-go proposition. That's a lot of fun but can also result in a lot of mistakes. You'll need to give yourself lots of shooting time and coverage and take time to rehearse as well. Mistakes are important because you'll learn lots from them, so don't be afraid to take on the challenge. If you turn yourself into an expert in this new platform (and others that may spring up), you'll be ahead of the game and become a valuable player in an emerging format.

You can tailor your short to reflect anything you want it to but remember—even in showcasing technical ability—story and character are everything. If those aren't honored, then no matter how good the technical work is, audiences will lose interest and stop watching, and that includes industry people you want to impress!

Reference

Unit 9. (2016). 25 Thoughts On Virtual Reality Filmmaking. Accessed February 17. https://www.unit9.com/project/25-thoughts-on-vr-filmmaking-by-anrick/.

10

BANKROLL

Lots of screen writers don't like to think about money unless they're getting it! The thought of having to pay for our visions sometimes is just too overwhelming, but if we want to be professional we've got to think about it and think about it very seriously. We've got to remember that show business is just that—a business. No matter how artistic we like to think we are, ultimately, we've got to be able to raise the capital required to get our projects off the ground. That's true of any business startup and therefore true for filmmakers.

Although writing seems to be one of the "cheaper" art forms, requiring only minimal tools, screenwriting in its final form (an actual film) isn't cheap at all. In fact, it's downright exorbitant.

It's necessary finally for screen writers to come to terms with the fact that they are duty bound to think of budget if they want to get their project seen. We've discussed how to do that during the writing process in Chapters 6 and 7, but when the writing is done, it's time to make the screenplay come to life by raising the money necessary for production. This isn't easy to do and requires learning a mind-set crucial to your success.

Roberta Colangelo, producer, distributor, contract administrator, and paralegal with over 15 years of deal-making experience in the international film and distribution market, has some really sage advice about fundraising for those writing shorts for production. I'll be referring to her advice in this chapter to help you negotiate the funding world.

First, you've got to establish a budget for your project. There are lots of books on budgeting so I won't get into how to do that. You can use the template in Movie Magic that will help you determine how much money you'll need.

As I've mentioned earlier, the average 7-minute short using free camera equipment can come in at about $4,000, but I've seen students budget their 10-minute projects for $17,000, and some, who I think are crazy, even have spent as much as $35,000 on their short films. To my mind these figures are far too high. If you're going to spend that much, you might want to consider putting it into producing a feature!

Once again, remember that a short is your calling card to help you raise money for the feature and to introduce you to the professional world. That means that although it needs to be high quality and professional, it doesn't need to throw the maximum amount of dollars up on the screen. People with high budgets usually rent expensive equipment, pay their cast and crew, and hire other professionals to dress up their productions. And, as we spoke about earlier, they often do that by neglecting story, which is all important.

Let's say you've arrived at a decent doable budget and you need to raise money. How do you do that? Let's look at some sources.

Personal Funds

Some people use their own money. They save up. That's an okay idea but always very risky. You should only invest money you are willing to lose. Chances are you'll never get that money back.

You need to really think about how much that personal money means to you. I've known people who have mortgaged their houses to pay for films and have been financially devastated.

Don't sell your valuables, hock your jewelry, or rent your dog! There are other ways.

Others go to family and friends. This is also very risky. Family members and friends need to realize that they will NEVER get their money back. Short films seldom recoup their investments. Aunt Sadie may think it's a fabulous idea to invest in your career because she believes you'll hit it big, but may write you out of her will when she discovers she's "lost" that huge chunk of cash when your film failed to win an Oscar! (And even if it did, you might still wind up broke.)

It's wise then to offer Aunt Sadie and the friends who've chipped in to fund you something in return other than cash. Perhaps they'd like a credit, a visit to the set, an invitation to the wrap party, and screening. You can offer some fun things but be careful. You don't want a *Bullets Over Broadway* scenario where your best friend Freddy's given you megabucks in return for you casting his untalented girlfriend in the lead.

And then there's the issue of creative control. A friend of mine had a wealthy dentist invest in his film and then was driven crazy when the dentist showed up on the set every day demanding creative changes. Make sure what you promise is deliverable and that your investor knows what he or she is getting into. Put things in writing so there will be no surprises. Friendly handshakes are great but have a way of disappearing from memories when there is no written agreement.

Because these personal funds are so problematic, you should look at some other ways of raising money. You've got to think big here and be bold. Think in terms of "contributions."

Contributions

Roberta Colangelo breaks these down into three categories.

Fiscal Sponsorships

You may never have thought of these as a possibility but think again. Many charitable organizations (501(c)(3) of the Internal Revenue Code) might be interested in what your story is about. Remember Chapter 2? That was all about knowing what your story was *really about*. Take a look at your ultimate message. For example, I had a student writing a story about a woman trapped in a cult. The message: cults are dangerous. That student can hunt down organizations that specialize in deprogramming cult members and perhaps receive fiscal sponsorship. The organization should want little in return except for a credit. (Again, remember the caveat of script involvement touched on in Chapter 2 and decide if you want to let the organization have creative input. Make sure you get that in writing.)

Most organizations are happy to remain uninvolved if they are on board with the values of the script and its execution. One of my students wrote a script about teenage suicide and was able to get a suicide prevention organization to fund his entire film. This is the real payoff for knowing what your film is *really about* and making that ultra important as you write the script.

Corporate Sponsorships

Here's another opportunity to get creative. Ms. Colangelo defines this as corporations giving money or materials directly to the project. This means that companies, anxious to endorse their products or build up their image in communities, might contribute to a project they think closely aligns them with positive values.

For example, if you have a script that's about depression, you might get a drug company to fund you in return for a thank you at the end or a "brought to you by" or "With Special Thanks" at the beginning. "Thank you" credits can mean a lot of publicity and promotion to companies, particularly in markets where they are not often featured. Because they are anxious to get access to these markets, they might just come up with some funds. To entice them, you might want to consider who your audience is, and we'll talk about that a little later on.

You might also get corporations to contribute products or services. For example, many of my students are able to get food for their shoots by acknowledging restaurants in their credits. Contributions like these can save you lots and lots of money.

You might also be able to get products (props) placed in your film for free. But make sure that these products are integral parts of the story. Legally, they have to be. You don't want your movie to look like a commercial. For example, if you write a script where a watch figures prominently, you might get a watch company to sponsor the film or at least give you the use of one of their fabulous watches. If a car is an integral part of your film, you might be able to get a company to let you use one for free.

In 2001 and 2002, BMW funded *The Hire*, a series of eight short films 8 to 10 minutes long each, produced for the Internet. A form of branded content, the shorts were directed by prominent filmmakers like Alejandro Gonzales Inarritu, John Woo, Ang Lee, Guy Ritchie, Tony Scott, and John Frankenheimer; featured Clive Owen, Gary Oldman, Don Cheadle, Mickey Rourke, and Madonna; and were chock full of BMWs. Although the cars played a prominent part in the films, they were never mentioned specifically. The scripts were written by a team at BMW's advertising agency with input from the directors. Anonymous Content produced the films. David Fincher executive produced.

Some companies may not want to make movies themselves like BMW did but would be happy to include their products in yours. Remember that marketing and promotion is the ultimate goal of these corporations, so you've got to convince them you can reach a definite audience.

Grants

Grants are usually a long shot but not impossible. You can find a link to grants that will give you application forms and the documents you will require at: http://www.filmdaily.tv/grants/short-film

Remember that grants are not a sure thing and may not fit your production schedule. And they may not be large enough to make a dent. They can, though, be important in other ways. If people hear that you got a grant from a particular group, they might be more willing to contribute to your project. If others have shown confidence in your project, people will want to get on board too.

Promotion, Marketing, and Crowdfunding

All of this can take place at the same time. The first thing you've got to realize is that crowdfunding involves promotion and marketing. In fact, crowdfunding and marketing go hand in hand. Ms. Colangelo is quick to point out the difference between promotion and marketing, and this difference is often something filmmakers who use crowdfunding don't get.

Promotion is letting people know your film exists. You can put it on social sites and let them know you're in need of cash to make it happen. But marketing is more widespread and requires more work. As Ms. Colangelo says, "It shows audiences the value of your film and tells them why they should contribute to it."

You should give your film a Facebook page and a website. Including strong, significant buzzwords your film addresses can move it higher on the Google search engine. You will also need to Tweet regularly, making sure that you can bring something new to your Twitter feed every day. If you just repeat yourself, people will ignore you. And be sure to use relevant hashtags that will tickle individuals and corporations looking for those subjects your film highlights.

All of this takes a significant amount of work and attention. Putting in the time will up your chances of reaching your financial goal.

A Marketing Must: Finding Your Audience

Before you start, you should take a look at The Seed & Spark online handbook *Crowdfunding for Independence*! Seed & Spark calls itself an "independent film community where filmmakers and audiences join forces to fund films" and offers this handbook free on their site (www.seedandspark.com). It tells you in a clear, no-nonsense way everything you need to do to fund your film. And it begins by telling you that the first thing you've got to do is build your followers by finding your core audience.

That core audience is made up of the people who will be supportive and happy to contribute to your movie. How do you find those people? Consider your subject matter—what your film is *really about*. If, for example, your film is about life in the jazz world, you need to search out people who are interested in jazz. Check out Internet groups and forums devoted to jazz and let them know about your film. If your film is about mental illness, seek out groups interested in that issue. These groups will add to your crowdfunding base and give you contributors that reach far beyond family and friends.

Seed & Spark also suggests that you might want to "interview" a group of people face to face, people who you believe your film was "made for." It even gives you the questions you need to ask these people. Ask them where they get their news, what music they listen to, what blogs they read, what organizations they belong to, where they spend their free time.

The answers they give will help you learn what you should be saying, where you should be saying it and who you should be contacting.

If four of the five people say they spend more time on Twitter than Facebook, you might want to spend more time trying to reach your crowd on Twitter than on Facebook. Read the blogs they are reading, pay attention to how their favorite bloggers talk to them . . . learn a lot of essential things not just about how to talk about what you're making but how to make it in the most efficient way for your audience.

(*Seed & Spark*, 2016, p. 5)

Fiscal and corporate sponsors want to know details about the audience apart from simple demographics. People of the same age, gender, ethnic background, social class, etc., may not necessarily have the same tastes. Seed & Spark gives the hilarious example of two different people from the same demographic. Both people were born in 1948, grew up in England, married twice, have two children, are successful in business, are wealthy, spend their winter holidays in the Alps, and like dogs. But one is Prince Charles and the other Ozzy Osborne! Obviously men with different tastes and proclivities!

So beware the demographic trap. Instead be able to zero in on the specific kinds of things your audience reverberates with (discovered through those interviews: music, themes, platforms, etc.) and be able to wax lyrical about them. Fiscal and corporate sponsors will be impressed by your ability to market your film, your hard work, and ability to deliver the goods and that will make them eager to contribute to your project.

Crowdfunding Platforms

Once you've found your audience, you're ready to engage crowdfunding platforms. There are over 400 of them and so you need to really research which ones are right for you. You might want to check out Hivewire.ca, a site specifically geared to explaining crowdfunding.

Keep in mind that all crowdfunding sites take a percentage of funds raised and charge a percentage for credit card contributions. Kickstarter, for example, is a creative and artistic, all-or-nothing site. If you don't get all the money you request, you get nothing! It claims that over 44 percent of projects on this site are successful, and they charge 5 percent plus a 3 to 5 percent processing fee.

Indigogo allows funding for every type of project, and according to Hivewire, 28 percent of their projects are successful. They have a fixed 4 percent fee plus 3 to 5 percent for processing. That means they take 4 percent if you reach your goal (with a 3 to 5 percent processing fee) and 9 percent if you do not reach it (plus a 3 to 5 percent processing fee), but you get to keep the rest of the money.

Seed & Spark is only for film. Only when you reach 80 percent of your goal do you get the money. They charge 5 percent (plus a 3 percent processing fee), but offer contributors a chance to pay the processing fee on behalf of the filmmaker.

It's your job to check out all the sites and their terms and choose the one that fits with you and your project. Each site has specific guidelines you're going to need to follow, and only you know what you're willing to do. It's a big job, but it's what you need to raise the money to fund your project.

Once you commit to your crowdfunding site, you will have to make a pitch video (various sites offer instructions on what to include in this), you'll have to cold call sponsors, and you'll have to network like crazy, but it's all part of getting your film out there. In fact, the process is so involved that a whole other book could be dedicated to it. But that's not the substance of this particular book. The aim here is just to get you introduced to the process and to encourage you to enter it, realizing it's a necessary step to get your script into production.

Don't allow yourself to be shy, daunted, or overwhelmed. Team up with people who can help you get over your deficiencies. Get a good producer. Take one step at a time. Make sure that you have an attorney on board who can help with all the legal documentation. Get accounting and tax advice. If you don't have the money to do these things, try some low-cost options: friends of the family, LegalZoom, college interns—be creative. But most of all, have confidence in yourself and your project and be able to transmit your excitement about it. People love enthusiasm and the opportunity to help someone fulfill a dream. It's up to you to make sure that dream is engaging, meaningful, and viable and that you come across as a competent, energetic mega-talent people will want to work with.

Reference

Seed&Spark (2016). "Crowdfunding for Independence." www.Seedandspark.com/education/crowdfunding.

11
GETTING SEEN

The Festival Circuit

Let's face it—every filmmaker intends to show at film festivals. Unfortunately, there are no guarantees that a film will make it into a festival. And then, of course, there are entry fees that stack up if you apply to many of them. The average filmmaker spends between $2,000 and $3,000 on submissions. But festivals are the first go-to if you want your work to be seen and taken seriously.

It will take a lot of work and deep-thought strategy to negotiate the festival world, but you'll need to do that if you want to make any headway in your career. And it's a given that career will involve getting feature films made. Because your short is your calling card (as we've talked about before), you'll want to use festivals to lay the groundwork for funding that feature and perhaps also getting other film work.

To get professional strategy advice tailor made for you, you may want to hire a film consultant to help you devise that strategy. For the big picture and important tips, I turned to film festival programmer and film consultant Thomas Ethan Harris, who has given a seminar on film festival strategy at Loyola Marymount University. Mr. Harris has 20 years of experience as a film consultant and former director of programming (Los Angeles Film Festival, Palm Springs International Short Film Festival). His client base includes numerous Academy Award winners. He knows what he's talking about. Harris said:

> [B]efore you submit to any film festival pause and say, if I get into this festival what good can come for my film or my career? Always ask yourself that. You need an incentive before you submit. Don't just submit blindly. You're going to spend so much money on entry fees that it isn't worth it.
>
> If you're playing your cards right and your goal is to work in the U.S. and make films, your targets at first should be North American Film festivals, because at these festivals (Toronto, Telluride, Tribeca, Sundance) you have the opportunity to go there with your short and meet somebody like an emerging producer who can actually help you make a feature. That isn't going to happen on the international festival circuit. Foreign countries want to help their own people. They are not interested in helping the American short film maker make a feature.
>
> There are community festivals—Florida, Savannah and so on that are great servers of their communities but what are you expecting to find there? You need an incentive to apply to those. For instance you might be shooting your feature just outside of Savannah. That's a reason to go so you can meet the Georgia film commission and maybe get funding. If your incentive is to have your family come and the festival is where they live that makes sense. If you want to go to Italy and travel, you might want to apply to foreign festivals just to do that but don't apply to foreign or community festivals just because you want to be seen on the red carpet with no hope of getting a feature made.

Film festivals are more expensive than most people think. You should know that if you do get in to bigger festivals, you have to go. You just can't send your film. Nobody is paying your way to these festivals so you should structure out how much money you can spend on submission fees and how you're going to get there. If you plan on staying five days at a festival, that's a good $5,000 from your own pocket. Often filmmakers don't think about how much they'll have to lay out to show up at their festival screens.

Thinking about your major incentive to get noticed and get a feature made, Harris advises people to apply to mainstream business festivals first. What are mainstream business festivals? They're festivals that play all forms of content: documentaries, features, shorts, animation. They play a little of everything and are attended by the film business community. Producers, production companies, development people, and distributors go there to look for talent. Business people don't usually go to genre festivals or shorts festivals. Harris says that short festivals do have business people from the shorts world, but the people that are going to help you fund your feature are not going to be at a shorts festival.

Here's Harris's list of mainstream business festivals in order of importance:

1. Toronto International Film Festival
2. Sundance Film Festival
3. South by Southwest
4. Telluride Film Festival
5. New York Film Festival
6. Tribeca Film Festival
7. Chicago International Film Festival
8. San Francisco International Film Festival
9. LA Film Festival
10. Cleveland Film Festival

It's difficult to get into these festivals because they don't take many shorts. Mr. Harris says:

[I]f you want to play the North American Business circuit and find yourself with your short not getting into Sundance, South by Southwest and Tribeca you know that you don't have what the business festivals are looking for. It gives you a clue. It doesn't mean that you can't get into the LA film festival or the AFI Festival but you might then want to change your strategy a little and move away from the North American Business festivals and think about the community festivals.

Many of these are Academy Award qualifying and very prestigious. They just don't have that business community draw.

Savannah for instance is a very wealthy festival and the only one in the world that pays for film maker travel and food. And you get to go to restaurants where all the famous journalists are eating so you can talk to them. Some of these community festivals are great places to be able to meet people. Sundance is a really hard place to meet people but for instance, the Sonoma Film Festival is usually attended by Francis Ford Coppola and he's approachable. San Francisco is like that too. You can hang out with people at these community festivals and they are great for networking.

There are two primary film festival seasons: winter/spring (January through early May) followed by fall (August through the beginning of November). Know this and time your festival release when your picture is getting done. If you finish your film in April, for example, hold it a little bit and try for the fall festivals.

You should also know that very few festivals want premier status (that is, showing a film for the first time anywhere). For instance, Harris says that 80 percent of the shorts at Sundance have been seen in other festivals first, so most festivals don't care when your film is played. Toronto International Film Festival and Tribeca Film Festival are both interested in premier status, and they will check to make sure, but that's usually reserved for features. When you see a festival that you haven't heard about tell you your short has to be a premier play, then that is a warning that festival isn't really good. For features, premier status is everything. Not for shorts! Short filmmakers can start anywhere. Try to play mainstream festivals first, followed by genre and major metropolitan areas.

Timing and planning is important. Let's say you play the great Austin Film Festival in October. Harris says you're not going to get accepted into South by Southwest in March. When you play a major metropolitan community, and sometimes when you play a state itself (Texas is very rigid with the higher-end festivals this way), you'll be limited. For example, if you play the Austin Film Festival you won't be playing the Houston Film Festival too. You'll probably be able to play major metro areas only once and lots of states too, so you've got to play the festivals that are most important for your emerging career first.

Harris cautions that even though some of the festivals will have these requirements online so you'll know not to submit, many festivals won't tell you. They'll take your money and make you ineligible, so do your homework.

Harris points out one exception. He says that if you play Los Angeles, there are two primary mainstream festivals: the LA film festival in June and American Film Institute (AFI) in November. You are not going to be playing both, but what might be possible is that you can play the LA Film Festival in June and turn around and play a genre film festival later in the year like a Latino film festival, Asian American film festival, or a gay film festival, but you can't do the reverse. For example, if you play an Asian American film festival in May, you're not going to turn around and play a major festival in June.

What Festivals Are Looking For

Harris (2007) reminds us that not every short is a festival movie. He believes that

> *festivals are looking for auteur driven shorts. Festivals want to feel the presence of the director and a film that says something, has a point of view and a narrative design. Film makers have to be willing to get into the trenches with their own point of view. It's about character and story and then how you visually interpret that and you have to figure out what expressive way you're going to shoot that. The actual visualization of film comes from knowing who your character is.*

He goes on to say that festivals want a film

> *that has a personal visual voice and not just performance and dialogue. Does the director know when to use a long take? Does the director understand not to reverse angle? Film festivals are looking for relatively high production value but not common stuff. Festivals are trying to find potential and the next great film maker.*

> *Production value is hard core important, especially at Sundance. Making the choice to shoot in a low quality if it's a choice—that's one thing but if you put yourself out there in a rag tag way, people won't have much tolerance for that. Shorts at bigger festivals are very professional[ly] made.*

The Running Time Rule

I keep harping on this, but it can't be said enough. No matter how many times I tell my students to keep it under 15 minutes, they chomp at the bit to stretch their film beyond that. Ultimately, if they do that, they sabotage any possibility of festival play.

Harris agrees:

The running time of your film does matter! The average running time on the mainstream business circuit is 12 and ½ minutes. At mainstream film festivals like Sundance there are six short programs and they want to have between 7–10 shorts per program. The minute you cross the 15 minute line you are not going to play many festivals just based on running time.

Rejection

Everyone gets rejection letters from film festivals. They're part of the "game" and shouldn't destroy you. Harris says that Sundance is among the most fairly programmed festivals because seven to eight shorts programmers boil down 1,000 films to 200, and all the programmers have to see those. Sundance plays only 60 to 70 shorts a year. Tribeca has two programmers, and they split all of their submissions. Most of the festivals work with unpaid interns, so don't feel bad when you get rejected because your film might have been rejected by one of those!

Working the Room

When you arrive at a festival, Harris says that one of the most important things you can do is introduce yourself to someone on the publicity team. Go to the press office. People are very busy and under lots of pressure, so just introduce yourself quickly and tell them if something comes up and they need a short filmmaker to do an interview, you're available no matter when or where. You could get a call at 4 a.m. so get ready.

He also suggests that you find the nearest FedEx office just in case you might meet someone who wants your film sent to them. Find a copy place and a quiet meeting place where you can talk to important people who show interest.

Make sure (as we've already pointed out in an earlier chapter) that you have your feature script written and with you. Harris agrees that there is no reason to get on the festival circuit unless you want to finance a feature. No one wants to finance another short! People will ask you what you are doing next. Telling them you're working on a feature script that will be finished in six months won't work. In six months they will have forgotten about you and your short and you will have missed the boat!

And remember that in mainstream festivals, feature filmmakers are kings. Not everyone there understands the value of shorts. That's why you should consider entering shorts festivals (DC Shorts, LA Shortsfest, Palm Springs International Shortfest, etc.). If your short has played at good shorts festivals, people will be impressed and that will up your street cred.

The key in all of this is to stay determined and enthusiastic. Don't be laid low by rejection, and make sure that you've budgeted for festival play in your fundraising efforts for your short.

Homework

Go online and make a list of all the community and genre festivals that apply to your projects. Be careful to consider the significance of these festivals and how you can use them to advance your career and your visibility. This will take time, but you need to carefully think about how you can take advantage of all aspects of the festival (location, population draw, public relations avenues) and apply these to your particular project.

The Ultimate: An Oscar

Admit it! Every one of us has at some time pictured ourselves holding that rare golden statue and stammering out an acceptance speech. Winning an Oscar for your short film is a surefire career launch. You can certainly apply to get into the running, but you've got to fulfill certain criteria.

First, the film can't be more than 40 minutes long. Since we've already said that films more than 15 minutes long won't get into festivals, that means shorts more than 15 minutes long that have won Oscars haven't played at many festivals but might have qualified in other ways.

According to the Academy Awards website (www.oscars.org), to be eligible for award consideration, a short film must fulfill one of the following qualifying criteria within two years of the film's completion date:

> *The picture must have been publicly exhibited for paid admission in [a] commercial motion picture theater in Los Angeles County for a run of at least seven consecutive days with at least one screening a day prior to public exhibition or distribution by any nontheatrical means. The picture must also appear in the theater listings along with the appropriate dates and screening time(s).*

The site also includes technical requirements for these screenings (e.g., 35 mm or 70 mm film, or in a 24 or 48 frame progressive scan Digital Cinema format with a minimum projector resolution, etc.).

This means that you'll have to rent time at a legitimate Los Angeles theater to show your short for a week. Usually your film will play at some ridiculous hour (7 a.m. or 3 a.m.) to an empty house, but it will have fulfilled the Academy exhibition requirements.

Unfortunately, the Academy says *that student films cannot qualify with a theatrical release.* But they can qualify if they win a qualifying award (best narrative short, etc.) at a competitive film festival. There is a Short Film Qualifying Festival list along with the prizes you'll need to win to be eligible that you can find online at the website (www.oscars.org). It's long and substantial and includes the LA Film Festival, The Palm Springs Festival, Sundance, and Santa Barbara Film Festival. The Academy warns that this list may change so make sure you get the most current information possible.

Another way that student films can qualify is to win a Gold, Silver, or Bronze Medal award in the Academy's Student Academy Awards Animation, Narrative, Alternative, or Foreign Film category competition.

If your film does qualify, it can't be exhibited publicly or distributed anywhere in any nontheatrical form until after its Los Angeles release. That means that it can't be screened before that on broadcast and cable television, PPV/VOD (pay-per view, video-on-demand), DVD distribution, or on the Internet. That's another reason you need to shun a YouTube release. You can show excerpts of the film totaling no more than 10 percent of its running time. That's so that if you did show a clip of your project in order to get funding on one of the crowdfunding sites, you won't be penalized.

You can get more details on the Academy website. These include technical data regarding sound and format, print requirements, dialogue or narration requirements (these must be substantially in English or the film must have English language subtitles), print markings, etc.

The site also cautions that *only* if your film receives a nomination can you refer to it in advertising and publicity materials. If your film is selected for the shortlist, you can't identify yourself as an "Academy Award Finalist."

If you're up to that challenge, then why not go for it? Imagine the roar of the crowd, the glitz and glamor, your weeping parents, and your sorry-she/he-dumped-you ex! It's a worthwhile dream and a just reward for all that hard work.

Other Venues

It's true that film festivals are usually the first go-to choice for getting eyes on your project, but let's say you applied to scads of festivals, blew your bankroll and still didn't get anywhere. There is hope. You can always try your luck online. Things are looking up in that arena.

On July 31, Ryan Faughnder writing in the LA Times asked "What if Hollywood's most profitable summer movie came not from a comic book, a best-selling novel or a video game, but from a viral video on YouTube?"

He went on to answer his own question giving as example "the tiny budget horror film *Lights Out*. The PG-13 movie was based on a three minute film from Sweden and made by a director no one had ever heard of. Yet the well-reviewed film grossed about $40 million in its first week of release, roughly eight times what it cost to produce."

Faughnder says that "the eye-popping success of *Lights Out* represents a potential watershed moment for studios looking to YouTube as a source of inexpensive, untapped talent and ideas."

He quotes Jeff Bock, box office analyst at Exhibitor Relations who says: "If you can get enough hits organically through YouTube, guess what, Hollywood will come calling. These online channels are the way that people are going to be discovered in the future."

Faughnder says "to transition to more traditional modes of filmmaking. YouTube itself has evolved from an outlet for home-made videos to a much bigger player in the entertainment world. The San Bruno, California-based, Google-owned video platform opened a 41,000-square-foot production facility in Playa Vista in 2012, and in October launched the new subscription service YouTube Red.

"For their part, major studios have been under pressure to reach younger audiences who aren't flocking to movie theaters like their parents did. They've attempted to leverage the popularity of YouTube's 'creator' community, to reach a fervent, digitally savvy audience. DreamWorks Animation, Lionsgate and Paramount Pictures have all invested in the growing space."

If you get enough hits (that means lots!), you'll get noticed, and you can also enter video contests. There are scads of online competitions and you can put it out on Vimeo too. If you're lucky enough to be one of the Vimeo staff picks you can really go far!

The key is to try all sorts of options. Get out there. Don't limit yourself and be bold. You need to be your biggest advocate. You can't be shy. Blow your film's horn because you believe in it and in yourself. If you've got something wonderful, let the world know!

Reference

Harris, Thomas Ethan. "Navigating Film Festival Seminar Series" at Loyola Marymount University.

12

BE A NINJA!

Screenwriting is a martial art! Think about it. Just like a martial art, screenwriting requires profound dedication, concentration, intense practice, willingness to fight, strength, and courage.

Screenwriting is not for sissies! Production is not for sissies! The entire film business is not for sissies! If you want to continue in that business in any meaningful way, you've got to learn some very important survival skills that will get you through the most painful times. Acquiring these skills isn't easy. It takes a lot of work, soul searching, and introspection to make yourself realize how you can avoid the slings and arrows sure to be hurled at you during intense inner and outer battles.

And yes, there are battles. The inner ones are the most subtle and intense. The biggest one is usually the fight with your own personal writing issues. These can be varied and intense, and they involve those pesky voices we hear in the middle of the night that tell us we are crazy to do what we're doing, that we are no good at it, that we'll never succeed, that anything to do with art will get us nowhere financially, that we'll end up homeless and alone because of our addiction to an inane art form.

We learn to listen to these voices from an early age. Our parents, our teachers, media, and even the world indoctrinate us against having an artistic career. We are told to prepare for the future by studying practical things like math, sciences, car mechanics, woodworking, cooking, and a plethora of things that could help us earn big dollars. We are told that doctors, lawyers, and business professionals are valued in our society above painters, poets, and scribes. And we've seen for ourselves how true that is when it comes to money.

Except we often don't think about what all those pooh-poohers of the arts fail to see—that a world without art would be dismal and unlivable. Artists are valuable in the extreme because they show us who we are and that showing has the power to inform, inspire, and delight. It's a power not to be taken lightly.

The first battle many of us have to fight is the determination to engage in an artistic pursuit in spite of naysayers and discouragers, and it's a battle not for the timid. Just as I outlined in Chapter 1, you've got to be pretty sure you want to be an artist above anything else. You've got to really examine your motives and your inner proclivities through introspection and concentration and then have the determination and courage to act on what you've discovered.

Some of what you discover can be your fear. Fear is a scary thing! It can paralyze you in spite of your motivation. So you've got to really analyze what you're afraid of. We've already touched on one of the most basic fears: survival. You could be afraid that you'd starve to death and end up homeless. That fear can be easily removed by logic and practicality. Make sure that you acquire some basic job skills—not to fall back on because I don't believe that you should go into something thinking you might fall back. Develop some skills that you can use to earn a living while you're doing art.

T.S. Eliot worked in a bank. Quentin Tarantino worked in a video store. Lots of other artists have made their living doing things other than their art while they were perfecting their passion. Doing your art should be your passion. That, and not financial gain, should be your motive. If your motive is financial gain, you're a manufacturer and not an artist!

The fear that you're not good enough can be overcome by relentless practice and honing your skills. If you're busy doing that you won't have time to be afraid you can't do something. Erase that fear by doing it.

I remember the first time I got hired to write a project. I knew nothing about the subject matter and felt daunted and cowed. But only for a moment. I had learned through my early work in journalism to put my head down and plunge into a story because doing that I'd learn as I went. Often screenwriting is a learn-as-you-go thing. When you get engaged in the story and the characters, you learn how to negotiate your way through the project. For me, that's the exciting part.

I tell my students it's like being in the jungle with only a penknife. You have to slash your way through relentlessly to get to the other side. It's really the fun part of writing—working out this puzzle that takes on a life of its own. But you have to begin and engage, and that takes simply facing those fears and doing the thing anyway.

Some time ago I wrote a piece for the Writer's Store Website called "Dare to Dream: Write Anyway." In that I said:

> [S]ometimes—no often—it gets especially hard to write. Sometimes it feels like it's impossible to put into words the substance of our dreams—when the wolf's at the door financially and emotionally, when life's got us down and we are depleted and discouraged. But it's especially during those times we have to keep the dream alive and write anyway.
>
> And that's because writing is the thing that makes us feel truly alive—that convinces us that we're doing something special and contributing to the intangible substance that has the power to elevate humanity. It's that act and that contribution that most often saves us from the illusion that life always gets the better of us—that we can be whipped, conquered, beaten down. It's when we think that the bad guys may be winning

that we've got to gird our loins and dream even harder. It's during those times when we've got to take action and write anyway.

Oh sure there may be those who tell us we're wasting our time—that getting anything out there is impossible, that we're insignificant in the face of Nobel laureates, Oscar nominees and people who have been writing since infancy. But those people don't know that our dreams are exactly like the dreams of prize-winners and big-time "professionals."

Because those of us who write dream in a glowing commonality. We dream in the arena of knowing that words and images matter. We dream in the knowledge that this creative process is magic and certain; that when done well it works on the writer and the reader in equally powerful proportions. We know what those nay-sayers don't know—that in the very act of dreaming we confirm our determination to make a supreme effort to do the impossible and create a world.

It's in the act of attempting the impossible that we may even tell ourselves that we're wasting our time—that our dreams are implausible or too flawed to come true. During those times, we may be faced with terrifying personal demons—with specters of former failures that rise to haunt and beat us back. Especially during those insecure and anxious times, we have to block our ears to our own terror, we have to turn our backs on the undermining parts of ourselves and write anyway.

Our fears make us doubt our own talent. We may find other writers who write better than we do—who write the way we want to write—who write the way we suspect deep down we can never write. When that happens, we have to be humble enough to learn from those writers. We must also re-evaluate our ideas about the nature of talent. We need to realize that some people are born with talent fully developed and that some people (most people in fact) are born with talent that's like a seed that must be nurtured and coaxed to reach maturity. We've got to respect the level of our talent, rejoice in it and develop it by overcoming our fears of inadequacy and writing anyway.

There may be those who tell us we don't know enough; that our lack of education precludes our right to write. That's when we have to educate ourselves, to learn more and to live our unique lives in a thoughtful and reflective way so that we can become wise enough to earn our writing. We have to own what we know and write anyway.

There are those who may tell us we don't have the skills we need to engage others. That's when we have to work hard to gain those skills. We've got to decipher the mystery of our craft; we've got to master vocabulary; we've got to refine our tools of structure and nuance and we do that by constant practice and writing anyway.

All this learning is a lot of work and it's time consuming just like writing is. Where do we find the time to learn what we need to know, to carry on relationships, to run households and, if we aren't earning our living by writing (and most writers don't), work full-time jobs and still write? Getting time to write may be even harder than writing but if we are determined to do it, something interesting happens. Time becomes fluid and stretchable. Suddenly there are open moments where there were none before. And if we determine that writing is as integral to us as brushing our teeth, we will get up earlier, go to bed later, rearrange our priorities, juggle the events of our day, carve out space and no matter how busy we are, we'll write anyway.

There are times when we don't feel like writing—when we're emotionally drained, tired, spent. There are times when we feel empty and wordless; when we feel discouraged and angry and when we're caught in the snare of "what's the use?" During those times, when we feel especially dry, we've got to prime the pump and write anyway. Even if we're turning out drivel, nonsense and nothing at all, we've got to keep our dream alive, sit down and force ourselves to write anyway. In that act of writing, we reaffirm our commitment to ourselves. When we write anyway, we are keeping our promises and even if we think what we're writing is ultimately garbage, we're working on realizing our dreams.

That's true even when we're stuck. Sometimes we hit a wall in what we're writing and we can't see our way around it. That's when we are tempted to chuck the project, go onto something new. But stuck times are only indicators that we need to work harder to solve problems. That's when we've got to be relentless and even more determined. We've got to approach our story from a different direction, experiment more and move beyond the box of our own thinking. Being stuck means that we need to think more creatively. We have to hold on and keep writing in order to find our way around the problem because sometimes the solution can only come if we write through it. Often, in the great jumble of writing that pushes us against a writing wall, a ladder will emerge to get us over. If the ladder doesn't emerge, in all that writing we might find the seeds of a new story because even when we fail we're making progress.

That's especially true when our work has been rejected. When the manuscript in which we've taken so much delight and pride has been sent back to us unread and unedited or when it's been sent back to us rewritten and edited to death. That's when we have to take a deep breath, move back from our work, re-read ourselves with an objective eye, and rethink our words and write anyway.

We've got to resist the temptation to run away, to forget the whole thing; let "them" win and have "their" own way and the thousands of other things we tell ourselves when we've been criticized. During those times especially, we've got to be like swans—the only beings that can actually separate milk from water while they are drinking. Like swans who drink only the milk and leave the water, we've got to learn to take the good from criticism, use it to our advantage and write anyway.

And when the feedback is good—when people sing our praises, tell us we're excellent, brilliant, wonderful and inspired. When we're lauded, applauded, rewarded and extolled, we've also got to stand back and recognize how much of this milk is water. We've got to remember during those times that nothing is ever perfect, that even the greatest writers still have lots to learn. Lots of good writers have been ruined just as much by effulgent praise as they have by cruel criticism. We've got to remember to take praise just as lightly as we take condemnation. We've got to be realistic about our own skills and abilities. We've got to go back to our work, no matter how successful we've become and write anyway.

We've got to be willing to work hard and never become complacent. We can't ever let down our guard. Sometimes this can be very painful—especially when we have to abandon our work. That can happen a lot. It happens when we discover that someone else has already written exactly what we're been planning to write; that someone "famous" is writing what we're currently writing; that the same story we've just worked on for years, has just been published by someone else. During those times, we've got to be strong enough to walk away from what we thought was our own original idea—sometimes after years of work. We've got to be strong enough to weather that heartbreak, move on, start a new project and write anyway.

During those times we've got to recognize that even though our stories may not be unique, the way we tell them can be. We've got to believe in our own uniqueness and find a way of expressing it uniquely and because that's not easy to do, we've got to recognize that we may fail sometimes. We have to therefore change the way we look at failure. Like Edison, we've got to consider that it might be a positive stepping-stone to great success and we've got to keep going in spite of it, pick ourselves up and write anyway.

When we do dare to express our own uniqueness, there may be those who disagree with us—sometimes violently so. There may be those who disparage us for our points of view and for our opinions. We may make people angry or sad. We may alienate friends and make enemies. But if we are sure of what we want to say and we hold to our own integrity and truth, then we have to keep on saying it and write anyway.

All of this takes great courage, stamina and willpower. But courage, stamina and willpower are all part of writing—tools just as integral as words or ideas. Courage, stamina and willpower give us the ability to realize our dreams even when we think we no longer dream them. These qualities are the subtle engines of our dream power put into motion by the impetus of our subconscious mind. We've got to recognize that they are integral parts of the writing life and we've got to use them every moment of every day and especially while we are dreaming and writing anyway. It's only by daring to dream, our relentless pursuit of those dreams, our determination to realize our dreams—it's only by never giving up and writing anyway that we become the kind of writers (and people) we want to be.

(Beker, 2016)

Swami Sri Yukteswar says "look fear in the face and it will cease to trouble you!" (*Autobiography of a Yogi* 1981, p. 104). That means you've got to analyze why you are afraid and through logic and understanding annihilate that fear and how you react to it.

The most daunting fear for any of us is usually the fear of rejection. No one likes to be rejected. It's hideously painful.

It's a universal thing and cuts us all to the quick. It can create anxiety, depression, and despair, and it can affect our self-esteem and stop us from embarking on or continuing in our career if we let it. Rejection in love is one of the prevailing themes in music, literature, and all great art. Humans are continually trying to learn how to cope with rejection in both personal and professional arenas.

Years ago, I gave a workshop on coping with rejection at the Writer's Guild of America West. There was standing room only, and most of the people there were very successful. They'd sold scripts that actually got made and had loads of credits. Even so, they were still struggling with ways in which rejection affected them and their work. Here's what I told them and what I tell all my students: TOUGHEN UP!

We've got to learn to be less sensitive and to take things less personally. We have to stop confusing our work with our selves. Admittedly, that's hard to do because our work, if it's good and meaningful, comes out of our core values, the things that we hold most dear. It involves how we see life, and what we want to say about it. But we have to understand that what we say shouldn't be confused with rejection of the way in which we say it.

For example, let's say your story centers on two guys who hang out on the Santa Monica Pier when they hear desperate and articulate cries for help. The cries are coming from a duck caught up in a beach barbeque. The ruthless grill-meisters are too drunk to realize the duck can talk. The guys rescue the talking duck and take him to their apartment where they spend months getting to know him, growing to love him, and teaching him poker.

Eager to show off their protégée they decide to drive to Vegas. Halfway there, their fiendish GPS goes berserk and advises them to take a right turn into the desert. Worshipers of the technological gods, they follow directions and eventually realize they are lost and out of gas. The temperatures are brutal. They begin to broil. Hours go by. They are starving and thirsty. Desperate and addled, the two guys kill and eat the duck! A clear case of duckaside!

What's the story about? Guys surviving in the desert? A brutal killing? A poker cartel gone bad? No the story is really about *betrayal*! That's obviously a core value that's important to you. Once you know that, you can easily see how many ways you can demonstrate that value, how many other stories you can come up with based on that. When you do that, if a studio executive doesn't like ducks, you can still write about betrayal in lots of other ways that might move that executive.

Remember the exercise in Chapter 2? I asked you to come up with images from your own life that related to themes that interested you—you could call those themes your core values. The images were different and could have resulted in different story ideas but the core theme or value remained intact. Once you've recognized that, you can create many different stories based on the thing that moves you most at the moment, and you'll be less attached to the idea you've decided to spend your time developing.

That certainly applies to projects in the pitch stage. But what happens if your project has been completed and is rejected? That's the time you've got to learn to separate yourself from the project enough to realize that the rejection is not personal. Don't confuse your ideas with your self! Your thoughts and ideas come out of you and are transformed into an art form, but they are NOT you and neither is the art form!

We often forget this because we tend to believe everything we think and we tend to believe that our thoughts are who we are, so, when they are proven wrong or are rejected, we find ourselves doubting our self-worth. When our work is rejected or morphed into something we don't recognize, we believe *we* are being rejected. But what's really being rejected is the shadow of our essence—a shadow we've cast in the sunshine moment of creating. People may hate that duck, but they don't hate you!

It's important also to remember that as creators, we are shape-shifting constantly so the shadows we cast—our ideas—can and do change even though they have the same essence. And our idea supply is infinite. We can never lose anything. How many of us have reworked or resurrected "old" ideas we may have had years ago because their time had finally come?

That doesn't mean we don't commit to an idea. We've already talked about how important it is to do that. But the moment we recognize that idea is no longer working for us or is unacceptable in a crucial way, we need to be able to reframe it, say it in a different way or to move on altogether. How many of us have moved on from old work that we now recognize wasn't as good as we first thought? We've got to learn fluidity if we're to survive in this collaborative business where collaboration often means giving up a piece or all of our idea or transforming it into something unrecognizable.

That's why it's important to do the interior work of learning who we are apart from our writing. We need to discover our real selves because the real self is the raw material we weave into something else that's got warp and weft. No sane person blames the sheep if a wool sweater's ugly!

We gain confidence through self-discovery. When we find out who we really are and what we need to say, no one can take that away from us. Then we can master the trick of being fully engaged in our creative process but at the same time detached from it because we know that we are something greater and more solid. Very Zen.

To do that we've sometimes got to jump off our personal cliffs and let go of our old notions of what we need to make us feel successful. If success to us means getting approval from people, if it means never having our work edited, if it means making a quick sale above anything else, then we've got to take another look at why that matters so much to us. Doing that will help us relate to the reality of the film business where approval, no editing, and quick sales are as rare as sushi.

William Faulkner was once asked why he wrote for the movies and he said, "I can say exactly what I want to 10,000 people or more or less what I want to 10 million and I chose the larger number!" He was aware that he could still get his essential vision across in another way and doing that was an estimable victory.

And finally, screenwriters have to understand that the world has changed. We can no longer be passive in our careers. We can no longer wait to be discovered. We've got to take action and get proactive. We've got to consider taking an active part in our own projects by filming them ourselves. That's easier to do than it has ever been. In the old days it was financially impossible. Technology has helped us by making it possible for every one of us to make a movie by providing affordable platforms and new distribution methods. Take advantage of everything and stop waiting around for someone to give you the keys to your career. Take action! Be bold! Be brave! Be strong! Be a ninja!

To recap:

- Face your fears and analyze them. Use logic and truth to make them disappear.
- Know intimately what your core values are and be able to define them for yourself.
- Make the delivery of those values adaptable and varied.
- Realize that any change to the way you express your core values is superficial and does not need to betray those values.

- Never confuse your real self with your work—they are two separate things. The work is only one version of the infinite possible expressions of your core values.
- Develop a rational, realistic, workable definition of success.
- Take action to get your screenplay made and seen.
- Write anyway.
- Do all these things with courage and grace and you'll have a fulfilling career no matter what.

References

Beker, Marilyn. *Dare to Dream - Write Anyway!* www.writersstore.com/dare-to-dream-write-anyway. Accessed 18 November 2016.

Yukteswar, Swami Sri. *Autobiography of a Yogi.* Los Angeles, Self Realization Fellowship, 1981.

For Product Safety Concerns and Information please contact our EU
representative GPSR@taylorandfrancis.com
Taylor & Francis Verlag GmbH, Kaufingerstraße 24, 80331 München, Germany

www.ingramcontent.com/pod-product-compliance
Lightning Source LLC
Chambersburg PA
CBHW070612300426
44113CB00010B/1500